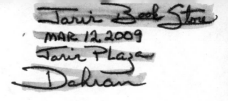

The
Essential
Arabic

The Essential Arabic

مَا يَلْزَمُ مِنَ الْعَرَبِيَّةِ

A Learner's Practical Guide

Rafi'el-Imad Faynan

GOODWORD BOOKS

First published 1998
Reprinted 2007
© Goodword Books 2007

Goodword Books Pvt. Ltd.
P O Box: 3244, Nizamuddin West,
New Delhi - 110 013
E-mail: info@goodwordbooks.com
Printed in India

www.goodwordbooks.com

For
my father and guru
Dr. K.A. Fariq

CONTENTS

PREFACE

The past three decades have witnessed the emergence of the Arab world as a centre of attraction and strategic importance for almost all countries of the world in general and the Third World in particular. This is due to significant developments not only in the industrial field but also in the socio-political milieu, which has created a situation of competition for capturing the West Asian markets and to establish economic and trade relations with the Arab countries. It is in this context that the interest in obtaining a sound knowledge of Arabic has increased considerably.

The teaching of Arabic language, particularly to non-Arabs, poses many challenges. When a teaching assignment commences, the teacher is invariably asked to recommend a book of grammar. If the course is to be successful and learner-friendly, it has to be a well-devised and graded one. The arrangement and sequence of lessons should be such that a learner moves forward step by step, from simple to complex structures. It is at this stage that he needs most to stand on firm ground. Anything confusing, lacking in precision and logical sequence may seriously diminish his interest and ability to comprehend. Unless such a book is sensitive to his need for precision and clarity, and unless it is successful in communicating the ideas effectively, both the teacher and the taught cannot be sure of good results. Although for learning a language, a good teacher with plenty of common sense, patience and hardwork is indispensable, the right choice of a grammar book plays an equally important role in bringing out the best in learners.

This volume covering the first half of the essential Arabic grammar is meant particularly for those learners who have lesser time at their disposal owing to their preoccupation in business and industry. A large number of such learners exists not only in

Asian and African countries but also in Europe and Latin America. They are the ones who know English as a second language and find it difficult to delve into lengthy and scholarly books. As there can be nothing new in a book of grammar except its presentation and its ability to effectively and smoothly communicate ideas to the mind of a beginner, this volume attempts to introduce in twenty lessons the first half of the essential aspects of Arabic grammar. The remaining half is to be presented in another volume. This book embodies the methods which I have found to be very effective while teaching grammar to beginners as well as those at an advanced level for over two decades. Still, much will depend on the teacher who must guide his pupils to make the best use of this small book.

Its main features are:

1. It exposes the learner only to the most basic and essential rules of grammar preparing him for those in greater detail later.
2. It unfolds the lesson by putting across one idea in one sentence enabling him to grasp the subject step by step.
3. It gives examples at the end of each lesson with grammatical analysis which, in charts, helps him identify each word facilitating quick comprehension.
4. It deals with the *dual* and the *plural* nouns and verbs only after the fifteenth lesson when he has learnt enough grammar using the singular and is now mature enough to grasp these too.
5. By giving explanations for the changes, it attempts to simplify the complex 'weak verbs' which puzzle the student most.

This book can cater to the needs of:
1. Beginners at any language school or college.
2. Short-term courses.
3. Graduate/Postgraduate students.

The following schedule may be followed:

Ist Semester

1. Introduction to Lesson 5 : First month (15 hours)
2. Lessons 6 to 10 : Second month (15 hours)
3. Lesson 11 : Third month (15 hours)
4. Lesson 12 : Fourth month (15 hours)

2nd Semester

5. Lessons 13 to 16 : Fifth month (15 hours)
6. Lessons 17 to 20 : Sixth month (15 hours)

For encouraging me to write this small book, I would like to express my gratitude to my father Dr. K.A. Fariq, Professor of Arabic, University of Delhi to whom it is dedicated. He has been the source of inspiration for me. Also to my Mother who, despite her agonizing bouts of depression, spared me some time, albeit very short, to give it final touches. I am thankful to my brother Mr. Ahmad Farhan, Lecturer in English, Jamia Senior Secondary School, New Delhi for his valuable suggestions. Also to my sister Ms. Firind Fariq, Lecturer in Arabic, School of Foreign Languages, Ministry of Defence, New Delhi for her most valuable suggestions. She was indispensable in checking the proofs.

I would also like to express my thanks to Mr. Saniyasnain Khan, the publisher of this book, who extended total support and cooperation without which this work would not have been possible.

Rafi'el-Imad Faynan
Professor of Arabic
Jamia Millia Islamia,
New Delhi

April, 22, 1998
24, Mujeeb Bagh,
Jamia Nagar,
New Delhi

THE ARABIC ALPHABET

Alpha-bet	English Symbol	Letter's Name	Initial	Medial	Final	Example	Pronunciation	With Definite Article	Pronunciation	Meaning
ا	a	Alif	ا		ـا	أَبٌ	Abun	الأَبُ	Al-Abu	The Father
ب	b	Baa'	بـ	ـبـ	ـب	بَيْتٌ	Baitun	الْبَيْتُ	Al-Baitu	The House
ت	t	Taa'	تـ	ـتـ	ـت	تُفَّاحٌ	Tuffaahun	التُّفَّاحُ	At-Tuffaahu	The Apple
ث	th	Thaa'	ثـ	ـثـ	ـث	ثَلاَّجَةٌ	Thallaajatun	الثَّلاَّجَةُ	Ath-Thallaajatu	The Fridge
ج	j	Jiim	جـ	ـجـ	ـج	جَمَلٌ	Jamalun	الْجَمَلُ	Al-Jamalu	The Camel
ح	ḥ	Ḥaa	حـ	ـحـ	ـح	حَافِلَةٌ	Ḥaafilatun	الْحَافِلَةُ	Al-Ḥaafilatu	The Bus
خ	kh	Khaa	خـ	ـخـ	ـخ	خَادِمٌ	Khaadimun	الْخَادِمُ	Al-Khaadimu	The Servant
د	d	Daal	د		ـد	دَرْسٌ	Darsun	الدَّرْسُ	Ad-Darsu	The Lesson
ذ	dh	Dhaal	ذ		ـذ	ذِئْبٌ	Dhibun	الذِّئْبُ	Adh-Dhibu	The Wolf
ر	r	Raa'	ر		ـر	رَجُلٌ	Rajulun	الرَّجُلُ	Ar-Rajulu	The Man
ز	z	Zaay	ز		ـز	زَهْرَةٌ	Zahratun	الزَّهْرَةُ	Az-Zahratu	The Flower
س	s	Siin	سـ	ـسـ	ـس	سَمَكٌ	Samakun	السَّمَكُ	As-Samaku	The Fish
ش	sh	Shiin	شـ	ـشـ	ـش	شَجَرٌ	Shajarun	الشَّجَرُ	Ash-Shajaru	The Tree
ص	ṣ	Ṣaad	صـ	ـصـ	ـص	صَبَاحٌ	Ṣabaahun	الصَّبَاحُ	Aṣ-Ṣabaahu	The Morning
ض	ḍ	Ḍaad	ضـ	ـضـ	ـض	ضَيْفٌ	Ḍaifun	الضَّيْفُ	Aḍ-Ḍaifu	The Guest
ط	ṭ	Ṭaa'	طـ	ـطـ	ـط	طَائِرَةٌ	Ṭaa'iratun	الطَّائِرَةُ	Aṭ-Ṭaa'iratu	The Airplane
ظ	ẓ	Ẓaa'	ظـ	ـظـ	ـظ	ظَبْيٌ	Ẓabyun	الظَّبْيُ	Aẓ-Ẓabyu	The Gazelle
ع	'a	'Ayn	عـ	ـعـ	ـع	عُشٌّ	'Ushshun	الْعُشُّ	Al-'Ushshu	The Nest
غ	gh	Ghayn	غـ	ـغـ	ـغ	غُرْفَةٌ	Ghurfatun	الْغُرْفَةُ	Al-Ghurfatu	The Room
ف	f	Faa'	فـ	ـفـ	ـف	فَاكِهَةٌ	Faakihatun	الْفَاكِهَةُ	Al-Faakihatu	The Fruit
ق	q	Qaaf	قـ	ـقـ	ـق	قُفْلٌ	Quflun	الْقُفْلُ	Al-Quflu	The Lock
ك	k	Kaaf	كـ	ـكـ	ـك	كُرْسِيٌّ	Kursiyyun	الْكُرْسِيُّ	Al-Kursiyyu	The Chair
ل	l	Laam	لـ	ـلـ	ـل	لِبَاسٌ	Libaasun	اللِّبَاسُ	Al-Libaasu	The Dress
م	m	Miim	مـ	ـمـ	ـم	مُدَرِّسٌ	Mudarrisun	الْمُدَرِّسُ	Al-Mudarrisu	The Teacher
ن	n	Nuun	نـ	ـنـ	ـن	نَافِذَةٌ	Naafidhatun	النَّافِذَةُ	An-Naafidhatu	The Window
ه	h	Haa'	هـ	ـهـ	ـه	هَاتِفٌ	Haatifun	الْهَاتِفُ	Al-Haatifu	The Telephone
و	w	Waaw	و		ـو	وَرْدٌ	Wardun	الْوَرْدُ	Al-Wardu	The Rose
ي	y	Yaa'	يـ	ـيـ	ـي	يَدٌ	Yadun	الْيَدُ	Al-Yadu	The Hand

THE INTRODUCTION

1 THE ALPHABET

(a) There are twenty nine characters in the Arabic alphabet :

1.	ا	11.	ز	21.	ق
2.	ب	12.	س	22.	ك
3.	ت	13.	ش	23.	ل
4.	ث	14.	ص	24.	م
5.	ج	15.	ض	25.	ن
6.	ح	16.	ط	26.	ه
7.	خ	17.	ظ	27.	و
8.	د	18.	ع	28.	ي
9.	ذ	19.	غ	29.	ء
10.	ر	20.	ف		

(b) They are written from right to left.

(c) Except ا, د, ذ, ر, ز and و all *can be joined* to the following letters.

(d) The first letter أَلِف serves two purposes

   (1) it elongates a consonant as in حَافِلَة (ḥaafilatun) and

   (2) it acts as the bearer of هَمْزَة (hamzatun) as in أَبٌ (abun).

2 THE PRONUNCIATION

2. (A)

   (1) Labial   : ف, و, م, ب

   (2) Interdental   : ذ, ث

   (3) Dental and Emphatic : ز, س, د, ت
        (Low Timbre)   ظ, ط, ض, ص

   (4) Frontal Palatal   : ر, ل, ن, ش, ج

12

(5)	Palatal		ك ,ي
(6)	Uvular (Tense. Deep)	:	غ , خ, ق
(7)	Pharyngeal	:	ح Sharp Whisper
			ع Compressed Sound
(8)	Junctional	:	ء Glottal Stop
			ه Breath

2. (B)

Other than the following, the letters are pronounced as in English:

(1) ء hamzah:

The glottal stop or catch. Its sound is produced by completely closing the vocal chords and then by suddenly separating them, as when the English word 'absolutely' is pronounced.

(2) ث : thaa :

The tip of the tongue touches the inside of the upper teeth. The sound resembles the unvoiced *th* of 'think'.

(3) ح : ḥaa :

The sound of ح is produced by a strong and sustained expulsion of breath. As when one breathes over the glasses to clean them.

(4) خ : khaa :

It is similar to the German 'ach'. The scrape, which is an essential of خ, is due to agitation of the velum (the soft palate) by the breath forced through the narrow orifice.[1]

(5) ذ : dhaal :

The tip of the tongue touches the inside of the upper

1.ʼ W. H. T. Gairdner, The phonetics of Arabic (Oxford 1925), P. 25.

13

teeth. Its sound resembles that of *'th'* in the English word 'that' or 'then'.

(6) ص : ṣaad :

ص is an emphatic 'ṣ' pronounced with the teeth slightly apart, pressing the tip of the tongue against the lower teeth and raising the tongue to press also against the upper teeth and the palate.[2]

(7) ض : ḍaad :

'Ḍaad' represents an "emphatic" velarized correlative of daal 'د', formed in the same way as is ص.[3]

(8) ط : ṭaa :

'Ṭaa' represents an "emphatic" velarized correlative of Ta 'ت', formed in the same way as is ص.[4]

(9) ظ : ẓaa :

Ẓaa represents an "emphatic" velarized correlative of dhaal ذ.[5] It is formed in the same way as is ص.

(10) ع : 'ayn :

'Ayn is a gutteral stop pronounced with constriction of the larynx.[6]

(11) غ : ghayn :

Ghayn is similar to the French 'r'. Its sound is close to that of gargling.

---

2. David Cowan, Literary Arabic (Cambridge 1925) p.3 and 4.
3. Farhat J. Ziadeh and R. Bayly Winder, An Introduction to Modern Arabic, (Princeton 1957) p.5
4. Farhat J. Ziadeh and R. Bayly Winder, An Introduction to Modern Arabic, (Princeton 1957) p.5.
5. Farhat J. Ziadeh and R. Bayly Winder, An Introduction to Modern Arabic, (Princeton 1957) p.5
6. David Cowan, Modern Literary Arabic (Cambridge 1958) p. 3 and 4.

(12) ق : qaaf :

'Qaaf' is a gutteral 'k' pronounced from the back of the throat.[7]

3 | THE VOWELS

There are two kinds of vowels :

(a) The short vowels

(b) The long vowels

(a) THE SHORT VOWELS

(1) There are three short vowels in Arabic :

    (i) Damma (u)

    (ii) Fatha (a)

    (iii) Kasra (i)

(2) Damma, the equivalent of *u* is written above a letter, e.g.

    تُ (tu),   جُ (ju),   نُ (nu) etc.

(3) Fatha, the equivalent of *a* is also written above a letter, e.g.

    تَ (ta),   جَ (ja),   نَ (na) etc.

(4) Kasra, the equivalent of *i* is written below a letter, e.g.

    تِ (ti),   جِ (ji),   نِ (ni) etc.

(5) All these three vowels are generally omitted in writing.

(b) THE LONG VOWELS

To form long vowels, damma, fatha and kasra are followed by the letter associated with them. Thus :

1. 'Damma' (u) is associated with و so it precedes واو to form a long vowel, e.g.

---

7. David Cowan, Modern Literery Arabic (Cambridge 1958) p.3 and 4.

تُو (tuu), جُو (juu), نُو (nuu) etc.

2. 'Fatḥa' (a) is associated with ا so it precedes أَلِف (alif) to form a long vowel, e.g.

تَا (taa), جَا (jaa), نَا (naa) etc.

3. 'Kasra' (i) is associated with ي so it precedes ياء to form a long vowel e.g.

تِي (tii), جِي (jii), نِي (nii) etc.

4 THE DIPHTHONGS

The two diphthongs: (i) 'au' as in 'jau', and (ii) 'ai' as in 'jai' are formed when fatha is followed by a vowelless و or ي. For example:

(i) جَوْ jau (ii) جَيْ jai

5 THE ORTHOGRAPHIC SIGNS

There are four orthographic signs :

(1) Sukuun

(2) Shadda

(3) Madda

(4) Tanwiin

1. **SUKUUN**

   The state of *being vowelless* is indicated by the symbol ◦ *over* a letter. For example :

   تَحْتَ (tahta), قُرْبَ (qurba) خَلْفَ (khalfa).

   In these examples, ح, رْ, and لْ are vowelless or *without movement.*

2. **SHADDA: THE DOUBLING SIGN**

   In Arabic, two similar letters coming one after another are *not*

16

written twice, instead a sign —͏ٌ, either called shadda or tashdiid, is placed *above* the letter written once. Example:

مَرَّ (marra) instead of مَرَرَ.

شَمَّ (shamma) instead of شَمَمَ.

3. MADDA : THE LENGTHENING SIGN

The sign ~ called 'madda' or 'lengthening sign' is placed above 'alif ' when it is to be elongated. The alif is *not* written twice. Examples :

آب (aab) instead of ا اب. آل (aal) instead of ا ال.

4. TANWIIN : THE 'NUNATION'

(1) In Arabic the nouns and adjectives are either definite or indefinite. The 'definite' noun like *the boy* in English is generally prefixed with 'the definite article.'

(2) Those nouns and adjectives which are indefinite like 'a boy' mostly carry a sign called 'tanwiin' (تَنْوِين) or 'nunation' on the *last letter* e.g. وَلَدٌ (a boy) waladun.

(3) This sign tanwiin (or nunation) is so called because it imparts a 'n' sound to the last letter of the word, e.g. وَلَدٌ (waladun).

(4) Tanwiin with 'ḍamma' is written as —͏ٌ *above* a letter, e.g. وَلَدٌ (waladun) 'a boy' or زَهْرَةٌ (zahratun) 'a flower'.

(5) Tanwiin with 'fatḥa' is written as —ً *over* أَلِف, e.g. وَلَدًا (waladan) 'a boy' (and not وَلَدً) بِنْتًا (bintan) 'a girl' (and not بِنتً).

The alif has to be brought to act as a *carrier* of this nunation except when a word ends with the 'round ة'. e.g. زَهْرَةً (zahratan) 'a flower' or حَافِلَةً (ḥaafilatan) 'a bus'.

(6) Tanwiin with 'kasra' is written as —ٍ *below* a letter. e.g. وَلَدٍ (waladin) 'a boy' or زَهْرَةٍ (zahratin) 'a flower'

(7) All these cases وَلَـدٌ, وَلَداً and وَلَدٍ mean 'a boy' that is *an indefinite* boy It is through the study of grammar one learns where to use anyone of these three cases.

6 THE DEFINITE ARTICLE

(1) In Arabic, the nouns and the adjectives are either 'definite' or 'indefinite'. Most indefinite words like 'a boy' generally carry 'tanwiin'.

(2) Those nouns and adjectives which are definite like *the boy* are prefixed with the definite article اَلْ (alif laam) called أَدَاةُ التَّعْرِيفِ (adaat ut-ta'riifi) e.g. اَلْوَلَدُ (al-waladu): 'the boy'.

(3) When a word is prefixed with اَلْ, it *cannot* carry tanwiin. Thus: وَلَدٌ is 'a boy'. And اَلْوَلَدُ *without* tanwiin is 'the boy'.

(4) When 'al' is prefixed to words beginning with the following letters, the 'ل' in 'al' is *not* pronounced, instead that letter is *doubled* as it is shown in the chart 'The Arabic Alphabet'. These fourteen are known as the *'sun letters'*:

ت, ث, د, ذ, ر, ز, س, ش, ص, ض, ط, ظ, and ن.

Examples:

زَهْرَةٌ (zahratun), 'a' flower, الزَّهْرَةُ (az-zahratu) 'the' flower.

شَجَرٌ (shajarun), 'a' tree, الشَّجَرُ (ash-shajaru) 'the' tree.

(5) The remaining fourteen letters with which 'ل' in 'al' is pronounced are called the 'moon letters'

7 THE CASES

(1) In Arabic, there are three cases called التَّشْكِيلُ (at-tashkiilu) or الشَّكْلُ (ash-shaklu).

(2) They are :

(a) Nominative case. e.g. وَلَدٌ – اَلْوَلَدُ (with ḍamma).

(b) Accusative case. e.g. وَلَداً – اَلْوَلَدَ (with fatḥa).

(c) Genitive case. e. g. وَلَدٍ – اَلْوَلَدِ (with kasra).

(3) Depending on its position in a sentence, a word can generally have any of three 'case endings' or 'vowel marks'. This *variation* of تَشْكِيلٌ on the *last letter* of an Arabic word like اَلْوَلَدُ, اَلْوَلَدَ and اَلْوَلَدِ is what one mainly studies in grammar.

8 THE GENDER

The nouns in Arabic are *either* masculine *or* feminine. Mostly the *absence* of the round ة called اَلتَّاءُ المَرْبُوطَـة (attaa ul-marbuuṭa) which is also called اَلتَّـاءُ المُـدَوَّرَة (attaa ul-mudawwara) shows that a noun is *masculine*. A large number of nouns and adjectives are turned into feminine *by suffixing the round* ة to them.

The 'masculine' is called: مُذَكَّرٌ (mudhakkarun). And the 'feminine' is called: مُؤَنَّثٌ (mu'annathun).

Example:

خَادِمٌ : (khaadimun) a male servant - خَادِمَةٌ : (khaadimatun) a maid servant.

مُدَرِّسٌ : (mudarrisun) a male teacher - مُدَرِّسَةٌ : (mudarrisatun) a lady teacher.

9 THE GRAMMAR

In Arabic grammar, one studies the coordination of particles, nouns and the verbs to form a sentence correctly by applying the right case ending called التَّشْكِيلُ or الشَّكْلُ on or below the *'last'* letter of a word.

اَلْمُبْتَدَأُ وَالْخَبَرُ
The Subject and the Predicate

EXAMPLE

The book	**is**	**new.**
(1)		(2)
↓		↓
SUBJECT (MUBTADA)		PREDICATE (KHABAR)

---

1. Observe the above sentence well.

2. In the above sentence we find that *'the book'* is a word about which something is being said. And it comes before *'is'*, so it is called 'the subject' or اَلْمُبْتَدَأُ (*al-mubtada'u*).

3. Then after *'is'* we find *'new'*. It is called 'the predicate' or اَلْخَبَرُ (*al-khabaru*).

4. In Arabic, there is no word for *'is'*, *'am'* or *'are'*.

5. The 'vowel mark' or التَّشْكِيلُ of اَلْمُبْتَدَأُ is *damma*. Hence: الْكِتَابُ. When we say التَّشْكِيلُ of اَلْمُبْتَدَأُ is (*damma*), we mean the 'vowel mark' of its *last* letter.

6. The تَشْكِيلٌ of الْخَبَرُ is also *damma*. Hence: جَدِيدٌ (It carries *no* alif laam).

7. If the 'subject' is masculine (مُذَكَّرٌ) then the 'predicate' must also be masculine.
   For example: اَلْكِتَابُ جَدِيدٌ (al-kitaabu jadiidun).

8. If the subject is feminine (مُؤَنَّثٌ) then the predicate must also be feminine. For example: The fridge is new: الثَّلَّاجَةُ جَدِيدَةٌ

(ath-thallaa-jatu jadii-datun).

This round ة, the symbol of a *feminine* noun, suffixed to الثَّلاَّجَةُ is what necessitated suffixing a similar ة to the predicate جَدِيدَةٌ to make it *feminine* too.

REMEMBER

(a)   that words like *'this'* and *'that'* are called the 'demonstrative pronouns' 'This' is هَذَا (haadha) for referring to someone 'masculine' and هَذِهِ (haadhihi) for 'feminine.' 'That' is ذَلِكَ (dhaalika) for 'masculine' and تِلْكَ (tilka) for 'feminine.'

(b)   When we say 'this chair', it is *definite*, therefore هَذَا alongwith اَلِـفْ and لَاَمْ has to be attached to the noun as هَذَا الْكُرْسِيُّ or as 'that car': تِلْكَ السَّيَّارَةُ (feminine: تِلْكَ plus the *definite* noun (السَّيَّارَةُ.

(c)   In a unit like هَـــذَا الكُرْسِـــيُّ (haadhal-kursiyyu), the 'demonstrative pronoun' هَذَا is called (اِسْمُ الإِشَارَةِ) (ismul-ishaarati) and اَلْكُرْسِيُّ is called الْمُشَارُ إِلَيْهِ (al-mushaaru ilaihi), meaning: something pointed to.

EXERCISE

Grammatically analyse the following sentences:

1.   The chair is comfortable.   :   اَلْكُرْسِيُّ مُرِيحٌ.
     Al-kursiyyu muriihun.

2.   The boy is bright.   :   اَلْوَلَدُ ذَكِيٌّ.
     Al-waladu dhakiyyun.

3.   This school is good.   :   هَذِهِ الْمَدْرَسَةُ جَيِّدَةٌ.
     Haadhihil-madrasatu jayyidatun.

4.   That car is beautiful.   :   تِلْكَ السَّيَّارَةُ جَمِيلَةٌ.
     Tilkas-sayyaaratu jamiilatun.

21

5. The teacher is busy.

Al-mudarrisu mash-ghuulun.

اَلْمُدَرِّسُ مَشْغُولٌ.

GRAMMATICAL ANALYSIS

That car *is* **beautiful.**

(1)   (2)

جَمِيلَةٌه   تِلْكَ السَّيَّارَةُ

(2)   (1)

↓   ↓

خَبَرٌ   مُبْتَدَأ

↓   ↓

التَّشْكِيلُ: ضَمَّة   التَّشْكِيلُ: ضَمَّة

↓   ↓

مُؤَنَّث   مُؤَنَّث

     ↓

     تِلْكَ:

     اِسْمُ الإشَارَةِ

---

(1) تِلْكَ السَّيَّارَةُ : is اَلْمُبْتَدَأ. Its تَشْكِيلٌ is damma. It is مُؤَنَّث and تِلْكَ is اِسْمُ الإشَارَةِ for referring to something feminine.

(2) جَمِيلَةٌ : is اَلْخَبَرُ. Its 'vowel mark' or تَشْكِيلٌ is also damma. Since اَلْمُبْتَدَأ is feminine, this too is suffixed with round ة (called: *attaa-al-mudaw-wara*).

INSTRUCTIONS

Memorize all the five sentences so that you translate them not only from English into Arabic but vice-versa too.

f-les

حُرُوفُ الْجَرِّ
The Prepositions

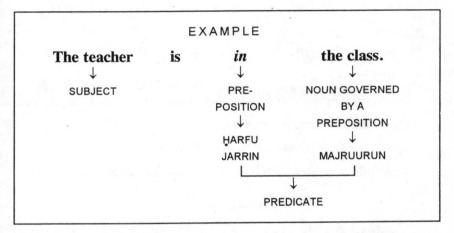

EXAMPLE

The teacher	is	*in*	the class.
↓		↓	↓
SUBJECT		PRE-POSITION	NOUN GOVERNED BY A PREPOSITION
		↓	↓
		ḤARFU JARRIN	MAJRUURUN

↓

PREDICATE

1. In English, the words like: *in, from, to, for* and *with* etc. are called *prepositions*.

2. In Arabic, these *prepositions* are called حُرُوفُ الْجَرِّ (*huruuf-ul-jarri*).

3. We know that most nouns in Arabic can have any of the *three* 'vowel marks'. For example the noun: 'the class' can be: اَلْفَصْلُ، اَلْفَصْلَ and اَلْفَصْلِ with no change in its meaning.

4. In Arabic, the noun coming *after* حَرْفُ الْجَرِّ gets *kasra* (كَسْرَةٌ) as its final 'vowel mark'.

5. And then, *the noun with kasra* is called مَجْرُورٌ (*majruurun*) meaning: 'the noun governed by a preposition'.

6. Thus the above sentence: 'The teacher is in the class' is to be translated as: اَلْمُدَرِّسُ فِي الْفَصْلِ

23

Here اَلْمُدَرِّسُ is الْمُبْتَدَأَ with damma as its تَشْكِيل or 'vowel mark'. And الْفَصْل is الْخَبَرُ which consists of فِي as حَرْفُ الْجَرِّ and اَلْفَصْل as مَجْرُورٌ the تَشْكِيل of which is كَسْرَةٌ and

7. Some prepositions (حُرُوْفُ الْجَرِّ) are:

In	=	فِي	(fi)	At/In	= بِ	(bi).
To	=	إِلَى	(ila)	Until/Till	= حَتَّى	(ḥatta).
On	=	عَلَى	('ala)	Since	= مُنْذُ	(mundhu).
From	=	مِنْ	(min)	About	= عَنْ	('an).
For	=	لِ	(li)	Like, as	= كَ	(ka).
With	=	مَعَ	(ma').			

8. In Arabic, most *feminine proper names* (like سُعَادُ ,فَرِيدَةُ ,فَاطِمَةُ etc.) neither accept *'nunation'* (تَنْوِيْنٌ) nor *kasra*. In case of *kasra*, they are given *fatha*. For example:

The child is sitting with Farida : اَلطِّفْلُ جَالِسٌ مَعَ فَرِيدَةَ.

ANALYSIS

اَلطِّفْلُ is الْمُبْتَدَأُ. And جَالِسٌ is اَلْخَبَرُ. Both of them carry تَشْكِيل of *damma*. مَعَ is حَرْفُ الْجَرِّ and فَرِيدَةَ is مَجْرُورَةَ the which should be *kasra* but as it is a woman's name therefore it gets *fatha* without nunation.

Mark that the preposition لِ is never written *detached* from مَجْرُورٌ. It is not written as: ل الْوَلَدِ , instead it is joined as in: لِلْوَلَدِ (lil-waladi: *for the boy*) or لِلْمَدْرَسَةِ (lil-madrasati: *for the school*).

The preposition مِنْ loses the سُكُوْنٌ on its *last letter* and instead gets فَتْحَةٌ when a noun with أَلِفٌ وَلاَمٌ is brought *after* it. For example:

مِنَ الْمَدْرَسَةِ (minal-mad-rasati): *from* the school.

مِنَ السُّوْقِ (minas-suuqi): *from* the market.

24

9. Re-read the above eight points before you attempt the exercise below.

EXERCISE

Grammatically analyse the following sentences:

(1) The student is going *to the school.* اَلتِّلْمِيذُ ذَاهِبٌ إِلَى الْمَدْرَسَةِ.

At-tilmiidhu dhaahibun ilal-madrasati.

(2) The girl is sitting *on the chair.* اَلْبِنْتُ جَالِسَةٌ عَلَى الْكُرْسِيِّ.

Al-bintu jaalisatun 'alal-kursiyyi.

(3) This bus is coming *from the college.* هَذِهِ الْحَافِلَةُ قَادِمَةٌ مِنَ الْكُلِّيَةِ.

Haadhihil-ḥaafilatu qaadimatun minal-kulliyati.

(4) That bus is going *to the university.* تِلْكَ الْحَافِلَةُ ذَاهِبَةٌ إِلَى الْجَامِعَةِ.

Tilkal-ḥaafilatu dhaahibatun ilal-jaami'ati.

(5) Ali is returning with Fatima *from the market.*

عَلِيٌّ رَاجِعٌ مَعَ فَاطِمَةَ مِنَ السُّوقِ.

'Aliyyun raaji'un ma'a Faatimata minas-suuqi.

GRAMMATICAL ANALYSIS			
This bus	**is coming**	**from**	**the college.**
(1)	(2)	(3)	(4)
الْكُلِّيَةِ.	مِنَ	قَادِمَةٌ	هَذِهِ الْحَافِلَةُ
(4)	(3)	(2)	(1)
↓	↓	↓	↓
مَجْرُورٌ	حَرْفُ الْجَرِّ	اَلْخَبَرُ	اَلْمُبْتَدَأُ
↓		↓	↓
اَلتَّشْكِيلُ:		اَلتَّشْكِيلُ:	اَلتَّشْكِيلُ:
كَسْرَةٌ		ضَمَّةٌ	ضَمَّةٌ
		↓	↓
		مُؤَنَّثٌ	مُؤَنَّثٌ

1. هَـٰذِهِ الْحَافِلَـٰةُ: is 'subject' or اَلْمُبْتَدَأُ. Its تَشْكِيلٌ is *damma*. It is feminine, so is the demonstration pronoun هَـٰذِهِ: 'this'.

2. قَادِمَـٰةٌ: is 'predicate' or اَلْخَبَرُ. Its تَشْكِيلٌ is also *damma*. It too has round ة called '*at-taa al-mudaw-wara*' suffixed because the 'subject' is feminine.

3. مِنْ: is a 'preposition' or حَرْفُ جَرٍّ (*harfu-jarrin*).

4. الْكُلِّيَةِ : is مَجْرُورٌ the تَشْكِيل of which is *kasra*.

INSTRUCTIONS

Orally analyse all the other sentences on this pattern.

اَلْمُبْتَدَأُ الْمُؤَخَّرُ وَالْخَبَرُ الْمُقَدَّمُ

The Delayed Subject and the Advance Predicate

E X A M P L E

In the house	*(there) is*	**a man.**
↓		↓
DEFINITE PREDICATE		INDEFINITE SUBJECT
↓		↓
AL-KHABARUL MUQADDAMU		AL-MUBTADA'UL MUAKH-KHARU

---

1. You have learnt that generally the word which comes 'before' *is* is called اَلْمُبْتَدَأُ and the information which comes 'after' it is called اَلْخَبَرُ as in 'The book is new': اَلْكِتَابُ جَدِيدٌ.

2. In Arabic, if اَلْمُبْتَدَأُ is 'indefinite' like 'a man' in: 'a man is in the house', it is brought *after* 'the definite' predicate.

3. Thus a sentence like: '*A man* is in the house', رَجُلٌ فِي الْبَيْتِ is *not* allowed; instead it is converted into 'In the house (there) is a man': فِي الْبَيْتِ رَجُلٌ (*fil-baiti rajulun*).

4. And then 'a man' is called 'the subject delayed' or اَلْمُبْتَدَأُ الْمُؤَخَّرُ (*al-mubtada ul-muakh-kharu*).

5. And 'in the house' which consists of حَرْفُ جَرٍّ and a definite مَجْرُورٌ is called 'the advance predicate' or اَلْخَبَرُ الْمُقَدَّمُ (*al-khabar ul-muqaddamu*).

6. In other words, 'the definite' in a prepositional sentence is to be brought *first*, even if it is *not so* in English.

EXERCISE

Grammatically analyse the following sentences:

1. There is a student in the class.
   (In the class there is a student).
   Fil-faṣli tilmiidhun.

   فِيْ الْفَصْلِ تِلْمِيذٌ.

2. There is a newspaper on the table.
   'Alaṭ-ṭaawilati jariidatun.

   عَلَى الطَّاوِلَةِ جَرِيدَةٌ.

3. There is a table in the room.
   Fil-ghurfati ṭaawilatun.

   فِي الْغُرْفَةِ طَاوِلَةٌ.

4. In the fridge there is an apple.
   Fith-thallaajati tuffaahatun.

   فِي الثَّلاَّجَةِ تُفَّاحَةٌ.

5. On the window there is a curtain.
   'Alan-naafidhati sitaaratun.

   عَلَى النَّافِذَةِ سِتَارَةٌ.

GRAMMATICAL ANALYSIS

On the window	there is a curtain.

(1)	(2)
سِتَارَةٌ.	عَلَى النَّافِذَةِ

(2)	(1)
↓	↓
مُبْتَدَأٌ مُؤَخَّرٌ	خَبَرٌ مُقَدَّمٌ
↓	↓
اَلتَّشْكِيلُ: ضَمَّةٌ	عَلَى: حَرْفُ الْجَرِّ
	↓
	النَّافِذَةِ: مَجْرُورٌ

---

1. عَلَى النَّافِذَةِ = Here you find that something is said about 'a curtain' which should be اَلْمُبْتَدَأُ and thus brought first. But since it is *'indefinite'*, therefore its appearance is *'delayed'*. Instead something *definite* like the prepositional sentence

28

اَلْخَبَرُ الْمُقَدَّم is brought *first* and is called عَلَى النَّافِذَةِ

2.   سِـتَارَةٌ = is اَلْمُبْتَـدَأُ but being *indefinite*, it is brought *after* the 'definite' خَـبَرٌ. Thus it is called اَلْمُبْتَدَأُ الْمُؤَخَّرُ whose تَشْكِيلٌ is *damma*.

INSTRUCTIONS

As there is a slight deviation here in the normal sequence of 'subject and predicate', you must grasp this by re-reading the lesson slowly and by grammatically analysing all the remaining sentences on this pattern.

اَلضَّمِيرُ

The Personal Pronoun
❦❧

1. The personal pronoun is called اَلضَّمِيـرُ : aḍ-ḍamiiru (plural: اَلضَّمَائِرُ)

2. The personal pronoun or اَلضَّمِيرُ is of *two* kinds:

   (a) ضَمِيرٌ مُنْفَصِلٌ (ḍamiirun munfaṣilun)

   (b) ضَمِيرٌ مُتَّصِلٌ (ḍamiirun muttasilun)

3. In English, words like: *he, she, you* and *I* etc. are called 'personal pronouns nominative'. In Arabic, it is called ضَمِيرٌ مُنْفَصِـلٌ (ḍamiirun munfasilun) and its تَشْكِيلٌ *never* changes: *he* remains: هُوَ ; *she* is هِيَ ; *you* is أَنْتَ, أَنْتِ and *I* is أَنَا .

4. In English, the words like *his, her, your* and *my* are called 'personal pronouns possessive' In Arabic such word is called ضَمِيرٌ مُتَّصِـلٌ (ḍamiirun muttasilun). And this ضَمِيرٌ مُتَّصِـلٌ is suffixed to a word.

5. Once this ضَمِيرٌ مُتَّصِلٌ is suffixed to a noun, it can neither carry *nunation* (تَنوِيـنٌ) nor *the definite article* (أَلِفٌ وَ لَاْمٌ). Just as it is incorrect to say '*a my book*' or '*the my book*'.

6. These ضَمَائِرُ مُـتَّصِلَةٌ carry fixed تَشْكِيلٌ except in case of 'his' where هُ as in كِتَابُهُ (his book), loses its *damma* and instead gets *kasra* whenever the letter *before* it is either سَاكِنٌ (vowelless) as in إِلَيْهِ or carries *kasra* as in كِتَابِهِ (kitaabihi).

7. Note that these ضَمَـائِرُ مُـتَّصِلَةٌ as they are given below in all *three* cases. You will find that their own تَشْكِيلٌ does *not*

change except in case of كِتَابِهِ.

(1) *His* = هُ as in كِتَابُهُ (his book)

كِتَابِهِ – كِتَابَهُ – كِتَابُهُ

(2) *Her* = هَا as in كِتَابُهَا (her book)

كِتَابِهَا – كِتَابَهَا – كِتَابُهَا

(3) *Your* (masculine) = كَ as in كِتَابُكَ (your book)

كِتَابِكَ – كِتَابَكَ – كِتَابُكَ

(4) *Your* (feminine) = كِ as in كِتَابُكِ (your *fem*. book)

كِتَابِكِ – كِتَابَكِ – كِتَابُكِ

(5) *My* (common) = ي as in كِتَابِى (my book)

كِتَابِي – كِتَابِي – كِتَابِي

8. The above examples demonstrate that ضَمِيرٌ مُتَّصِلٌ carries a fixed 'vowel mark' irrespective of its position in a sentence. The only exception is هُ which becomes هِ in case the letter *before* it carries *kasra* as in فِي سَـيَّارَتِهِ (in his car), or if it is سَاكِنٌ (vowelless) as in إِلَيْهِ (to him).

9. The حَرْفُ الْجَرِّ : ل undergoes a change of تَشْكِيلٌ and gets فَتْحَةٌ when it is *prefixed* to these ضَمَائِرُ مُتَّصِلَةٌ : لَهُ (for him), لَهَا (for her), لَكَ (for 'you' masc.) لَكِ (for 'you' fem.). But it retains its *kasra* when prefixed to ي as in لِي (for me).

EXERCISE

Grammatically analyse the following sentences:

(1) *His office* is far from his home.　　مَكْتَبُهُ بَعِيدٌ مِنْ بَيْتِهِ.

Maktabuhu ba'iidun min baitihi.

(2) She is busy in *her office*.　　هِيَ مَشْغُولَةٌ فِي مَكْتَبِهَا.

Hiya mashghuulatun fii maktabihaa.

31

(3) Is *your (masc.) school* closed?
Hal madrasatuka mughlaqatun?

هَلْ مَدْرَسَتُكَ مُغْلَقَةٌ؟

(4) No, *his college* is closed.
La, kulliyatuhu mughlaqatun

لَا، كُلِّيَتُهُ مُغْلَقَةٌ.

(5) *My father* is working in his room.
Waalidii 'aamilun fii ghurfatihi.

وَالِدِي عَامِلٌ فِي غُرْفَتِهِ.

GRAMMATICAL ANALYSIS

مَكْتَبِهَا.	فِي	مَشْغُولَةٌ	هِيَ
(4)	(3)	(2)	(1)
↓	↓	↓	↓
مَجْرُورٌ	حَرْفُ جَرٍّ	خَبَرٌ	مُبْتَدَأٌ
↓		↓	↓
هَا: ضَمِيرٌ مُتَّصِلٌ		تَشْكِيلٌ: ضَمَّةٌ	ضَمِيرٌ مُنْفَصِلٌ
		↓	↓
		مُؤَنَّثٌ	مُؤَنَّثٌ

---

(1) هِيَ: is مُبْتَدَأٌ. Had it been a noun its تَشْكِيلٌ would have been *'damma'*. But since it is ضَمِيرٌ مُنْفَصِلٌ its تَشْكِيلٌ is a 'fixed *fatha*'.

(2) مَشْغُولَةٌ: is خَبَرٌ. Its تَشْكِيلٌ is ضَمَّةٌ. And it agrees with مُبْتَدَأٌ in being feminine.

(3) فِي: is a preposition or حَرْفُ جَرٍّ.

(4) مَكْتَبِهَا: مَجْرُورٌ or 'noun governed by *kasra*'. It has ضَمِيرٌ مُتَّصِلٌ referring to 'her' suffixed to it.

INSTRUCTIONS

Orally analyse all the remaining sentences on this pattern.

اَلْمُضَافُ وَ الْمُضَافُ إِلَيْهِ
The Construct State

EXAMPLE

The book	*of*	Majid is new:	مَاجِدٍ جَدِيدٌ	كِتَابُ
↓	↓	↓	↓	↓
Part: 1	Part: 2		MUḌAAFUN ILAIHI	MUḌAAFUN
↓	↓		↓	↓
مُضَافٌ	مُضَافٌ إِلَيْهِ		مُضَافٌ إِلَيْهِ	مُضَافٌ
↓	↓			
1. No nunation	1. With kasra			
2. No alif lam				

---

1. Any sentence which contains the word *of* belongs to this lesson.

2. The word which comes *before* 'of' is called the *possession* and in Arabic it is called اَلْمُضَافُ (al-*muḍaafu*).

3. The مُضَافٌ (muḍaafun) *cannot* carry nunation (تَنْوِينٌ).

4. The مُضَافٌ *cannot* have 'the definite article' (أَلْ).

5. It may carry *any of the three* case endings (تَشْكِيلٌ) as the need be.

6. Even though the مُضَافٌ cannot have أَلِفٌ وَلَامٌ, it is to be treated 'definite' because it belongs to someone or something.

7. The word which comes *after* 'of ' is called the *possessor* and in Arabic it is known as اَلْمُضَافُ إِلَيْهِ (al-*muḍaafu ilaihi*) and its

تَشْكِيلٌ is *kasra*. It may be given either nunation or the definite article أَلِفٌ لَامٌ as the need may be.

8. Thus the above sentence will be: كِتَابُ مَاجِدٍ جَدِيدٌ.

9. In case مُضَافٌ إِلَيْهِ comprises a *feminine proper name* like فَاطِمَةُ, the vowel mark will then be *fatha* without nunation, as we have already seen that such names neither accept *kasra* nor *tanwiin*. For example:

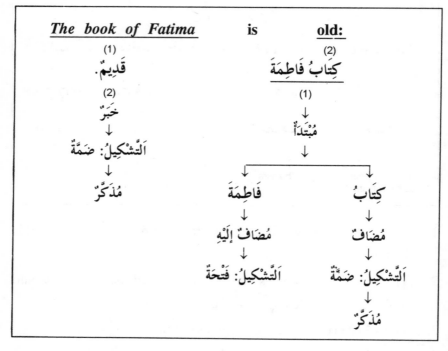

The book of Fatima   **is**   <u>**old:**</u>

1. كِتَابُ فَاطِمَةَ : كِتَابُ is مُبْتَدَأٌ. Its تَشْكِيلٌ is ضَمَّةٌ. It consists of كِتَابُ which is مُضَافٌ which can neither have the definite article أَلْ nor the تَنْوِينٌ. It is masculine. فَاطِمَةَ is مُضَافٌ إِلَيْهِ which should have كَسْرَةً but as it is a lady's name it is given *fatha without nunation*.

2. قَدِيمٌ: is خَبَرٌ (predicate) whose gender is determined only by كِتَابٌ which is مُضَافٌ.

34

EXERCISE

Grammatically analyse the following sentences:

1. The garden of the university is big and beautiful.

حَدِيقَةُ الْجَامِعَةِ كَبِيرَةٌ وَجَمِيلَةٌ.

Ḥadiiqatul-jaami'ati kabiiratun wa jamiilatun.

2. The colour of his car is beautiful.　لَوْنُ سَيَّارَتِهِ جَمِيلٌ.

Launu sayyaaratihi jamiilun.

3. The television of Farida is in her room. تِلْفِزْيُونُ فَرِيدَةَ فِي غُرْفَتِهَا.

Tilfizyuunu Fariidata fii ghurfatihaa.

4. The head of the department is sitting in his office.

رَئِيسُ الْقِسْمِ جَالِسٌ فِي مَكْتَبِهِ.

Raiisul-qismi jaalisun fii maktabihi.

5. He is going to the house of his friend. هُوَ ذَاهِبٌ إِلَى بَيْتِ صَدِيقِهِ.

Huwa dhaahibun ila baiti ṣadiiqihi.

GRAMMATICAL ANALYSIS

هُوَ	ذَاهِبٌ	إِلَى	بَيْتِ	صَدِيقِهِ.
(1)	(2)	(3)	(4)	(5)
↓	↓	↓	↓	↓
مُبْتَدَأٌ	خَبَرٌ	حَرْفُ جَرٍّ	مَجْرُورٌ	مُضَافٌ إِلَيْهِ
↓	↓		↓	↓
ضَمِيرٌ مُنْفَصِلٌ	اَلتَّشْكِيلُ: ضَمَّة		مُضَافٌ	اَلتَّشْكِيلُ: كَسْرَة
↓	↓			↓
مُذَكَّرٌ	مُذَكَّرٌ			ضَمِيرٌ مُتَّصِلٌ: ه

---

1. هُوَ :is ضَمِيرٌ مُنْفَصِلٌ and مُبْتَدَأٌ for *masculine singular*. Its vowel mark should be *damma* but as it is a personal pronoun, it carries a fixed تَشْكِيلٌ that is: *fatha*.

2. ذَاهِبٌ: is خَبَرٌ the تَشْكِيلٌ of which is *damma*. As the subject is

35

masculine (مُذَكَّرٌ), it too is masculine.

3. إِلَى: is حَرْفُ جَرٍّ or a preposition.

4. بَيْتِ صَدِيقِهِ: is مَجْرُورٌ in which بَيْتِ is مُضَافٌ, *devoid* of nunation or the definite article (اَلْ).

5. صَدِيقِهِ: is مُضَافٌ إِلَيْهِ whose تَشْكِيلٌ is *kasra* and it is suffixed with a ضَمِيرٌ مُتَّصِلٌ or 'personal pronoun possessive'. This pronoun is originally هُ but as the letter *before* it is carrying *kasra*, it too is given *kasra*.

INSTRUCTIONS

Orally analyse all other sentences on this pattern.

اَلْمَوْصُوفُ وَالصِّفَةُ

The Noun Qualified and The Adjective

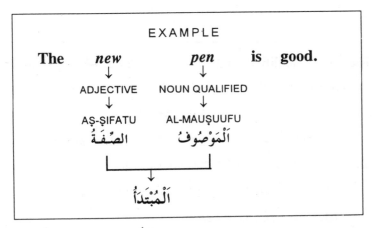

EXAMPLE

The   *new*   *pen*   is   good.
         ↓   ↓
    ADJECTIVE   NOUN QUALIFIED
         ↓   ↓
    AṢ-ṢIFATU   AL-MAUṢUUFU
    الصِّفَةُ   اَلْمَوْصُوفُ

اَلْمُبْتَدَأُ

1. In this example the مُبْتَدَأ consists of two words: 'The new pen'.

2. 'The *new*' in English is *'the adjective'*. In Arabic it is called الصِّفَةُ (aṣ-ṣifatu).

3. *'Pen'* in English is *'the noun'* or *'the noun qualified'*. In Arabic it is called اَلْمَوْصُوفُ (al-mauṣuufu). It is that noun for which an adjective is being used.

4. As you observed in this example, the 'adjective' or صِفَةٌ in English occurs *'first'* and then comes 'the noun qualified' or the مَوْصُوفٌ as 'the new pen'.

5. But in Arabic, the 'noun qualified' or اَلْمَوْصُوفُ is brought *first* and 'the adjective' or الصِّفَةُ *later*.

6. Thus the sentence: 'The new pen is good' is translated as:

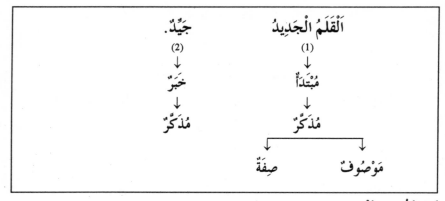

7. The noun qualified and the adjective i.e. اَلْمَوْصُوفُ and اَلصِّفَةُ have to *agree* with each other in four respects:

   (a) both *must have* the same تَشْكِيلٌ like:

   اَلْقَلَمُ الْجَدِيدُ – اَلْقَلَمَ الْجَدِيدَ – اَلْقَلَمِ الْجَدِيدِ

   (b) both *must either* be definite or indefinite, as:

   اَلْقَلَمُ الْجَدِيدُ – اَلْقَلَمَ الْجَدِيدَ – اَلْقَلَمِ الْجَدِيدِ

   (definite: *The new pen*).

   قَلَمٌ جَدِيدٌ – قَلَمًا جَدِيدًا – قَلَمٍ جَدِيدٍ

   (indefinite: *A new pen*).

   (c) both *must either* be masculine or feminine:

   masculine: اَلْوَلَدُ الصَّغِيرُ (the small boy).
   feminine: اَلْبِنْتُ الصَّغِيرَةُ (the small girl).

   (d) both must agree in number, as:

   in اَلْقَلَمُ الْجَدِيدُ, the مَوْصُوفٌ is *singular* and so is the صِفَةٌ.

8. Note that when تَنْوِينٌ in فَتْحَةٌ is to be given to a masculine word, an additional أَلِفٌ is to be suffixed to its last letter e.g. قَلَمًا جَدِيدًا (qalaman jadiidan).

9. If there are *more* than one adjective, they are brought in the following sequence:

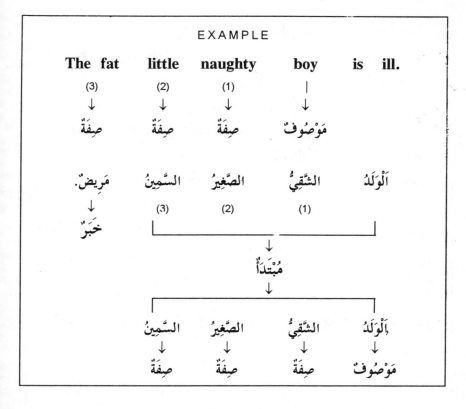

EXAMPLE

The fat	little	naughty	boy	is	ill.
(3)	(2)	(1)			
↓	↓	↓	↓		
صِفَة	صِفَة	صِفَة	مَوْصُوفٌ		

مَرِيضٌ.	السَّمِينُ	الصَّغِيرُ	الشَّقِيُّ	اَلْوَلَدُ
↓	(3)	(2)	(1)	
خَبَرٌ				

↓
مُبْتَدَأٌ
↓

السَّمِينُ	الصَّغِيرُ	الشَّقِيُّ	اَلْوَلَدُ
↓	↓	↓	↓
صِفَة	صِفَة	صِفَة	مَوْصُوفٌ

EXERCISE

Grammatically analyse the following sentences:

(1) The new teacher is a tall man.

اَلْمُدَرِّسُ الْجَدِيدُ رَجُلٌ طَوِيلٌ.

Al-mudarrisul-jadiidu rajulun ṭawiilun.

(2) The little girl is playing in the beautiful garden.

اَلْبِنْتُ الصَّغِيرَةُ لَاعِبَةٌ فِي الْحَدِيقَةِ الْجَمِيلَةِ.

Al-bintuṣ-ṣaghiiratu laaʿibatun fil-ḥadiiqatil-jamiilati.

(3) The new stadium is far from the house of my friend.

الإِسْتَادُ الْجَدِيدُ بَعِيدٌ مِنْ بَيْتِ صَدِيقِي.

Al-istaadul jadiidu baʿiidun min baiti ṣadiiqii.

(4) The little boy is naughty but intelligent.

اَلْوَلَدُ الصَّغِيرُ شَقِيٌّ وَلَكِنْ ذَكِيٌّ.

Al-waladuṣ-ṣaghiiru shaqiiyun walakin dhakiyyun.

(5) The sick man is going to the clinic of his village.

الرَّجُلُ الْمَرِيضُ ذَاهِبٌ إِلَى عِيَادَةِ قَرْيَتِهِ.

Ar-rajulul-mariiḍu dhaahibun ila 'iyaadati qaryatihi.

GRAMMATICAL ANALYSIS

	صَدِيقِى. (6)	بَيْتِ (5)	مِنْ (4)	بَعِيدٌ (3)	الْجَدِيدُ (2)	اَلإِسْتَادُ (1)
	↓	↓	↓	↓	↓	↓
	مُضَافٌ إِلَيْهِ	مَجْرُورٌ	حَرْفُ جَرٍّ	خَبَرٌ	صِفَةٌ	مُبْتَدَأٌ
	↓	↓		↓	↓	↓
	ضَمِيرٌ مُتَّصِلٌ: ي	مُضَافٌ		اَلتَّشْكِيلُ: ضَمَّةٌ مُذَكَّرٌ	اَلتَّشْكِيلُ: ضَمَّةٌ	اَلتَّشْكِيلُ: ضَمَّةٌ
				↓ مُذَكَّرٌ		↓ مَوْصُوفٌ ↓ مُذَكَّرٌ

---

(1) الإِسْتَادُ الْجَدِيدُ : *Both* of them make مُبْتَدَأ with the first word مَوْصُوفٌ being الإِسْتَادُ.

(2) الْجَدِيدُ : is صِفَةٌ. It agrees with مَوْصُوفٌ (الإِسْتَادُ) in all the *four* aspects:

    (a) both have the same 'vowel mark' (تَشْكِيلٌ),

    (b) the same gender,

    (c) the 'definite article' and

    (d) the same number.

(3) بَعِيدٌ : is خَبَرٌ (the predicate), the تَشْكِيلٌ of which is *damma*. It is masculine because اَلْمُبْتَدَأ is masculine.

(4) مِنْ : is حَرْفُ جَرٍّ which gives kasra to the word *after* it. It has a

fixed تَشْكِيلٌ which is سُكُونٌ.

(5) بَيْتِ صَدِيقِي : is مَجْرُورٌ in which بَيْتِ is مُضَافٌ which neither accepts 'nunation' nor 'the definite article'.

(6) صَدِيقِي = is مُضَافٌ إِلَيْهِ, the تَشْكِيلٌ of which is *kasra*. It is also suffixed with ي the ضَمِيرٌ مُتَّصِلٌ.

INSTRUCTIONS

Go through this lesson several times and grammatically analyse all the sentences on this pattern.

اَلْفِعْلُ الْمَاضِي * وَالْفَاعِلُ * وَالْمَفْعُولُ

The Past Tense Verb * The Doer * The Object

<table>
<tr><td colspan="3" align="center">EXAMPLE</td></tr>
<tr><td align="center">Majid</td><td align="center">wrote</td><td align="center">a book.</td></tr>
<tr><td align="center">↓</td><td align="center">↓</td><td align="center">↓</td></tr>
<tr><td align="center">DOER</td><td align="center">PAST TENSE
VERB</td><td align="center">OBJECT</td></tr>
</table>

1. The *past tense* verb is called اَلْفِعْلُ الْمَاضِي.

    اَلْفِعْلُ الْمَاضِي denotes 'action' that took place in the past like:

    He *wrote* = كَتَبَ

    He *read* = قَرَأَ

3. The *'person'* doing or taking part in this action is called 'the doer' or اَلْفَاعِلُ (al-faa'ilu) as *'Majid'* in 'Majid wrote'.

4. The تَشْكِيلٌ of اَلْفَاعِلِ is *damma*. For example: كَتَبَ مَاجِدٌ.
    ↓
    فَاعِلٌ

5. The *'object'* on which the *effect* of this verb *falls* is called اَلْمَفْعُولُ (al-maf'uulu) or اَلْمَفْعُولُ بِهِ (al-maf'uulu bihi).

6. The تَشْكِيلٌ of اَلْمَفْعُولُ is *fatha*.

7. Thus: "Majid wrote a book" becomes:

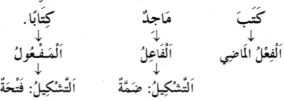

42

8. As 'the doer' مَاجِدٌ is a proper name, it does not need اَلْ. In the absence of اَلْ, مَاجِدٌ must have تَنْوِينٌ with damma: كَتَبَ مَاجِدٌ.

9. In Arabic, the *word order* for a verbal sentence can either be:

   (1) *verb–doer–object* e.g. كَتَبَ مَاجِدٌ كِتَابًا *or*

   (2) *doer–verb–object* e.g. مَاجِدٌ كَتَبَ كِتَابًا. *Both* are correct but the (1) *verb–doer–object* order is considered better.

10. In Arabic, the nature of verb is quite different from that of English.

11. In English, the verb '*wrote*' can stay as it is whether the 'doer' is masculine or feminine, singular or plural.

12. But in Arabic, the past tense varies. The past tense كَتَبَ (he wrote) is considered to be the '*original*' or the '*starting point*' in which certain *suffixes* are added to get the desired *gender* and *number*. Thus the 'starting point' كَتَبَ (he wrote) has *fourteen* patterns. These fourteen moods or patterns form the conjugation which is as follows:

THE CONJUGATION OF اَلْفِعْلُ الْمَاضِي

1.	كَتَبَ	He wrote (masculine singular)	Suffix	NIL
2.	كَتَبَا	Two men wrote	Suffix	الف
3.	كَتَبُوا	More than two/ many men wrote	Suffix	وا
4.	كَتَبَتْ	She wrote (feminine singular)	Suffix	تْ
5.	كَتَبَتَا	Two women wrote	Suffix	تَا
6.	كَتَبْنَ	Many women wrote	Suffix	نَ
7.	كَتَبْتَ	You (masculine singular) wrote	Suffix	تَ
8.	كَتَبْتُمَا	You (masculine dual) wrote	Suffix	تُمَا
9.	كَتَبْتُمْ	You (masculine plural) wrote	Suffix	تُمْ
10.	كَتَبْتِ	You (feminine singular) wrote	Suffix	تِ

11.	كَتَبْتُمَا	You (feminine dual) wrote	Suffix	تُمَا
12.	كَتَبْتُنَّ	You (feminine plural) wrote	Suffix	تُنَّ
13.	كَتَبْتُ	I (common) wrote	Suffix	تُ
14.	كَتَبْنَا	We (common) wrote	Suffix	نَا

13. The أَلِفٌ at no. 3, كَتَبُوا is *not pronounced* though it *must* be written. It is called أَلِفُ الْوِقَايَةِ *(the alif of protection)* or the *'otiose alif'*. It 'protects' verbs like أَخَذُوا (they took) where the و is not joined to the body of the verb and therefore may be mistaken for the conjunction و meaning '<u>and</u>'

14. In this conjugation, we find that numbers 1 to 6 indicate the *third person* masculine and feminine; 7 to 12 indicate the *second person* masculine and feminine and 13-14 indicate the *first person* (common).

15. Note that once the desired suffix is attached to the *original* كَتَبَ, *no* ضَمِيرٌ مُنْفَصِلٌ is required, for example in: '*she* wrote', there is no need to bring هِيَ as pattern number 4 كَتَبَتْ with its suffix of vowelless ت *contains* the meaning of هِيَ.

16. The masculine فَاعِلٌ must have *masculine* فِعْلٌ as in قَرَأَ مَاجِدٌ. The feminine فَاعِلٌ must have feminine فِعْلٌ as in قَرَأَتْ عَائِشَةُ.

17. To negate اَلْفِعْلُ الْمَاضِي, the word مَا called حَرْفُ النَّفْيِ is placed *before* it, irrespective of the number or gender. For example:
She did *not* write = مَا كَتَبَتْ   *or*
Majid did *not* read that book: مَا قَرَأَ مَاجِدٌ ذَلِكَ الْكِتَابَ.

18. If a word in Arabic has *sukuun* on its last letter as in ذَهَبَتْ (she went) *indicating no movement* and it is followed by a noun with the definite article اَلْ, then the سُكُونٌ is *replaced* by كَسْرَةٌ in order to avoid break in its pronunciation and to facilitate movement and flow. As in: ذَهَبَتِ الْبِنْتُ (dhahabatil-bintu).

44

Note that Arabs replace this سُكُونْ with كَسْرَةٌ only, and *not* with فَتْحَةٌ or ضَمَّةٌ.

(The only exception to the above rule is the preposition مِنْ which also has سُكُونْ on its last letter. But when a noun with أَلِفٌ و لاَمٌ is brought, it gets فَتْحَةٌ and *not* كَسْرَةٌ as in: مِنَ الْجَامِعَةِ (minal-jaami'ati). It will be incorrect to read it: مِنِ الْجَامِعَةِ (minil-jaami'ati).

19. For the expression '*has* or *have* written' the word قَدْ called حَرْفُ التَّوْكِيدِ is brought *before* الْفِعْلُ الْمَاضِي irrespective of number or gender. For example:

She *has* written   = قَدْ كَتَبَتْ *or*

They *have* written   = قَدْ كَتَبُوا

20. When ضَمَائِرُ like *him, her, you* and *me* come *after* a verb as مَفْعُولٌ (as in: He took *me*). they become:

(1)   هُ = for *him* as in: أَخَذَهُ إِلَى الْمَدْرَسَةِ.

He took *him* to the school.

(2)   هَا = for *her* as in: أَخَذَهَا إِلَى الْكُلِّيَّةِ.

He took *her* to the college.

(3)   كَ = for *you* as in: هَلْ أَخَذَكَ إِلَى الْمَكْتَبِ؟

Did he take *you* to the office?

(4)   كِ = for *you* (fem.) as in: هَلْ ضَرَبَتْكِ وَالِدَتُكِ؟

Did your mother beat *you*?

(5)   نِي = for *me* (common) as in   أَخَذَنِي وَالِدِي إِلَى السُّوقِ.

My father took *me* to the market.

Note that these ضَمَائِرُ are *joined* to the *verb* in the 'word order' of *verb/object pronoun/doer*. It is incorrect to *separate* the ضَمِيرٌ as مَفْعُولٌ from the verb as: أَخَذَ وَالِدِي نِي إِلَى السُّوقِ.

Give greater attention to this aspect and memorize the five

45

above mentioned examples.

20. Some past tense verbs for the exercise below are:

(1) أَكَلَ = he ate.

(2) فَتَحَ = he opened.

(3) ذَهَبَ = he went.

(4) جَلَسَ = he sat.

(5) أَخَذَ = he took.

EXERCISE

Grammatically analyse the following sentences:

1. The teacher has <u>written</u> the lesson on the blackboard.

قَدْ كَتَبَ الْمُدَرِّسُ الدَّرْسَ عَلَى السَّبُّورَةِ.

Qad katabal mudarrisud-darsa 'alas-sabbuurati.

2. The peon <u>did not open</u> the door of the class.

مَا فَتَحَ الْفَرَّاشُ بَابَ الْفَصْلِ.

Maa fataḥal-farraashu baabal-faṣli.

3. The girl <u>sat</u> on her desk and <u>read</u> the new lesson.

جَلَسَتِ الْبِنْتُ عَلَى مَكْتَبِهَا وَقَرَأَتِ الدَّرْسَ الْجَدِيدَ.

Jalasatil-bintu 'ala maktabihaa wa qara'atid-darsal-jadiida.

4. The little boy <u>took</u> the fruit from the fridge.

أَخَذَ الطِّفْلُ الصَّغِيرُ الْفَاكِهَةَ مِنَ الثَّلَّاجَةِ.

Akhadhaṭ-ṭifluṣ-ṣaghiirul-faakihata minath-thallaajati.

5. I <u>went</u> to the house of my teacher in the morning.

ذَهَبْتُ إِلَى بَيْتِ مُدَرِّسِي فِي الصَّبَاحِ.

Dhahabtu ila baiti mudarrisii fiṣ-ṣabaaḥi.

GRAMMATICAL ANALYSIS

(1)	(2)	(3)	(4)	(5)	(6)
أَخَذَ	اَلطِّفْلُ	الصَّغِيرُ	الْفَاكِهَةَ	مِنَ	الثَّلاَّجَةِ.
↓	↓	↓	↓	↓	↓
اَلْفِعْلُ الْمَاضِي	اَلْفَاعِلُ	صِفَةٌ	مَفْعُولٌ	حَرْفُ جَرٍّ	مَجْرُورٌ
	↓	↓			
	مُذَكَّرٌ	مَوْصُوفٌ			
		↓			
		مُذَكَّرٌ			

1. أَخَذَ = اَلْفِعْلُ الْمَاضِي is for third person/masculine/singular since the فَاعِل is masculine singular.

2. اَلطِّفْلُ = is اَلْفَاعِلُ and اَلْمَوْصُوفُ. Its تَشْكِيلٌ is damma.

3. الصَّغِيرُ = اَلطِّفْلُ الصَّغِيرُ is a part of اَلْفَاعِلُ. It is the صِفَةٌ which *agrees* with اَلْمَوْصُوفُ in being singular, in having same تَشْكِيلٌ, in being مُذَكَّرٌ and in being definite.

4. اَلْفَاكِهَةَ = is اَلْمَفْعُولُ, the تَشْكِيلٌ of which is *fatha*.

5. مِنْ = is حَرْفُ جَرٍّ.

6. الثَّلاَّجَةِ = is مَجْرُورٌ: a noun governed by a preposition.

MORE GRAMMATICAL ANALYSIS

My father took me to the market.

(1)	(2)	(3)	(4)
أَخَذَنِي	وَالِدِي	إِلَى	السُّوقِ.
↓	↓	↓	↓
اَلْفِعْلُ الْمَاضِي	اَلْفَاعِلُ	حَرْفُ جَرٍّ	مَجْرُورٌ
↓	↓		
ضَمِيرٌ مُتَّصِلٌ	ي: ضَمِيرٌ مُتَّصِلٌ		
↓			
مَفْعُولٌ			

47

1. اَلْفِعْلُ الْمَاضِي is أَخَذَ = أَخَذَنِي for the third person masculine singular. نِي is the ضَمِيرٌ مُتَّصِلٌ and مَفْعُولٌ. It is *never separated* from the verb. It is *never* brought *after* the فَاعِلٌ.

2. وَالِدِي = is فَاعِلٌ and ي is ضَمِيرٌ مُتَّصِلٌ (for: my). When this ي :ضَمِيرٌ مُتَّصِلٌ is suffixed to a noun, *no damma is allowed*. It *cannot* be وَالِدِيٌ.

3. إِلَى = is a 'preposition' (حَرْفُ جَرٍّ).

4. السُّوقِ = is مَجْرُورٌ or *'a noun governed by a preposition'*. Its case ending is كَسْرَةٌ.

INSTRUCTIONS

(1) Memorize the conjugations.

(2) Analyse all the remaining sentences on this pattern.

(3) Thoroughly pick up the ضَمَائِرُ when they happen to be مَفْعُولٌ.

اَلْفِعْلُ الْمُضَارِعُ

The Present Tense Verb

✵﴾❀﴿✵

EXAMPLE

Majid	**writes**	**a letter.**
↓	↓	↓
'DOER'	PRESENT TENSE VERB	OBJECT

---

1. The present tense verb is called: اَلْفِعْلُ الْمُضَارِعُ (al-mudaari'u).

2. اَلْفِعْلُ الْمُضَارِعُ denotes 'action' that is taking place *now* like:

   He *reads* = يَقْرَأُ

   He *writes* = يَكْتُبُ

3. The *doer* is called اَلْفَاعِلُ, the vowel mark of which is *damma* and the '<u>object</u>' is called اَلْمَفْعُولُ, the تَشْكِيلٌ of which is *fatha*.

4. In Arabic, each past tense verb has a particular فِعْلٌ مُضَارِعٌ, therefore the exact vowel marks of each one of them must be kept in mind. For example: كَتَبَ it is قَرَأَ as مُضَارِعٌ, and for يَقْرَأُ it is يَكْتُبُ

   Note the تَشْكِيلٌ of the *third* letter in يَكْتُبُ.

5. Like اَلْفِعْلُ الْمَاضِي, there are *fourteen* moods in the conjugation of اَلْفِعْلُ الْمُضَارِعُ.

6. In this conjugation, certain *prefixes* and *suffixes* are used *together* or *separately* to get the desired number and gender.

7. The conjugation of اَلْفِعْلُ الْمُضَارِعُ is as follows:

(1) يَكْتُبُ : He writes: *prefix* يَ.

(2) يَكْتُبَانِ : Two men write: *prefix* يَ and *suffix* انِ.

(3) يَكْتُبُونَ : More than two men write: *prefix* يَ and *suffix* ونَ.

(4) تَكْتُبُ : She writes: *prefix* تَ.

(5) تَكْتُبَانِ : Two women write: *prefix* تَ and *suffix* انِ.

(6) يَكْتُبْنَ : Many women write: *prefix* يَ and *suffix* نَ.

(7) تَكْتُبُ : You (masc. singular) write: *prefix* تَ.

(8) تَكْتُبَانِ : You (masc. dual) write: *prefix* تَ and *suffix* انِ.

(9) تَكْتُبُونَ : You (masc. plural) write: *prefix* تَ and *suffix* ونَ.

(10) تَكْتُبِينَ : You (fem. sing.) write: *prefix* تَ and *suffix* ينَ.

(11) تَكْتُبَانِ : You (fem. dual) write: *prefix* تَ and *suffix* انِ.

(12) تَكْتُبْنَ : You (fem. plural) write: *prefix* تَ and *suffix* نَ.

(13) أَكْتُبُ : I (common) write: *prefix* أَ.

(14) نَكْتُبُ : We (common) write: *prefix* نَ.

8. The masculine فَاعِلٌ must have masculine مُضَارِعٌ as in: يَقْرَأُ مَاجِدٌ. And the feminine فَاعِلٌ must be preceded by a feminine مُضَارِعٌ as in فِعْلٌ تَقْرَأُ الْبِنْتُ.

9. To negate اَلْفِعْلُ الْمُضَارِعُ, the word لا called حَرْفُ النَّفْي is brought *before* it. For example:

The girl does *not* read: لاَ تَقْرَأُ الْبِنْتُ.

10. اَلْفِعْلُ الْمُضَارِعُ contains the meaning of *future* in itself alongwith *present* but prefixing it with سَ س or سَوْفَ reserves it for *future*. For example: The student *will* write: سَيَكْتُبُ التِّلْمِيذُ or سَوْفَ يَكْتُبُ التِّلْمِيذُ.

11. For the expression *may* write, the word قَدْ is placed *before* اَلْفِعْلُ الْمُضَارِعُ for example : I *may go* to his house : قَدْ أَذْهَبُ

قَدْ تَكْتُبُ إِلَيْهِ. Or: she *may* write to him: إِلَى بَيْتِهِ.

12. The following verbs in both the past and the present tense should be memorized. The *third* letter of each فِعْلٌ مُضَارِعٌ should be given particular attention as it is there that the تَشْكِيلٌ changes.

(1)   To write: يَكْتُبُ   ⟵   كَتَبَ

(2)   To open: يَفْتَحُ   ⟵   فَتَحَ

(3)   To sit: يَجْلِسُ   ⟵   جَلَسَ

(4)   To read: يَقْرَأُ   ⟵   قَرَأَ

(5)   To live: يَسْكُنُ   ⟵   سَكَنَ

EXERCISE

Grammatically analyse the following sentences:

(1) Ayesha <u>sits</u> on the chair and <u>reads</u> the new lesson.

تَجْلِسُ عَائِشَةُ عَلَى الْكُرْسِيِّ وَتَقْرَأُ الدَّرْسَ الْجَدِيدَ.

Tajlisu 'Aayeshatu 'alal-kursiyyii wa taqra'ud-darsal jadiida.

(2) The peon will <u>open</u> the gate of the office in the morning.

سَوْفَ يَفْتَحُ اَلْفَرَّاشُ بَابَ الْمَكْتَبِ فِي الصَّبَاحِ.

Saufa yaftahul-farraashu baabal maktabi fiṣ-ṣabaaḥi.

(3) Do you <u>live</u> in that big house?

هَلْ تَسْكُنُ فِي ذَلِكَ الْبَيْتِ الْكَبِيرِ؟

Hal taskunu fii dhaalikal-baitil-kabiiri?

(4) Do you <u>read</u> and <u>write</u> Arabic in your class?

هَلْ تَقْرَأُ وَتَكْتُبُ الْعَرَبِيَّةَ فِي فَصْلِكَ؟

Hal taqra'u wa taktubul-'arabiyyata fii faṣlika?

(5) Majid does not <u>live</u> in this house.

لاَ يَسْكُنُ مَاجِدٌ فِي هَذَا الْبَيْتِ.

Laa yaskunu Maajidun fii haadhal-baiti.

51

GRAMMATICAL ANALYSIS

سَوْفَ (1)	يَفْتَحُ (2)	اَلْفَرَّاشُ (3)	بَابَ الْمَكْتَبِ (4)	فِي (5)	الصَّبَاحِ. (6)
↓	↓	↓	↓	↓	↓
حَرْفُ الْاِسْتِقْبَالِ	اَلْفِعْلُ الْمُضَارِعُ	اَلْفَاعِلُ	مَفْعُولٌ	حَرْفُ جَرّ	مَجْرُورٌ
	↓	↓	↓		
	لِلْمُذَكَّرِ	اَلتَّشْكِيلُ	مُضَافٌ		
		↓	↓		
	ضَمَّةٌ		مُضَافٌ إِلَيْهِ		

1. سَوْفَ = is called *'particle of future tense'* or حَرْفُ الْاِسْتِقْبَالِ (ḥarful-istiqbaali).

2. يَفْتَحُ = is اَلْفِعْلُ الْمُضَارِعُ in third person singular and masculine because the 'doer' is masculine.

3. اَلْفَرَّاشُ = is اَلْفَاعِلُ, the تَشْكِيلٌ of which is *damma*.

4. بَابَ الْمَكْتَبِ = is اَلْمَفْعُولُ, the تَشْكِيلٌ of which is *fatha*. بَابَ is مُضَافٌ and اَلْمَكْتَبِ is مُضَافٌ إِلَيْهِ with *kasra* as its vowel mark.

5. فِي = is a *preposition*.

6. الصَّبَاح = is a *noun governed by a preposition*.

INSTRUCTIONS

Practise all the five verbs on the patterns of the conjugation. Memorize اَلْفِعْلُ الْمُضَارِعُ of each past tense verb concentrating on its *third letter* as the next grammar lesson will depend on it.

LESSON NINE

فِعْلُ الأَمْرِ
The Imperative Verb
࿔

EXAMPLE

Go to your room: اِذْهَبْ إِلَى غُرْفَتِكَ.
↓ ↓
THE IMPERATIVE فِعْلُ الأَمْرِ
VERB

---

1. The *'imperative verb'* is called فِعْلُ الأَمْرِ (*fi'lul-amri*). It is a verb through which we *order* or *request* someone to do something. For example:

   Go (order) or *Please go* (request).

2. اَلْفِعْلُ الْمُضَارِعُ is derived from فِعْلُ الأَمْرِ.

3. If the *second* letter of اَلْفِعْلُ الْمُضَارِعُ is *vowelless* (سَاكِنْ), أَلِفٌ is introduced as *prefix* for فِعْلُ الأَمْرِ.

4. This *prefix* أَلِفٌ can have only <u>two</u> 'vowel points'. Either *damma or kasra*.

5. If the *third* letter of اَلْفِعْلُ الْمُضَارِعُ has *damma*, then we give *damma* to this أَلِفٌ, if not, then it is given *only kasra*.

6. And the 'last' letter of فِعْلُ الأَمْرِ is given سُكُونْ.

7. Thus the فِعْلُ الأَمْرِ from يَكْتُبُ where the *third* letter has *damma*, is اُكْتُبْ. Here we find that the *second* letter of اَلْفِعْلُ is كَافٌ and it is *vowelless* so we introduce أَلِفٌ for making فِعْلُ الأَمْرِ. In order to determine the تَشْكِيلٌ of this أَلِفٌ,

53

we observe the *third* letter. We find that it has *damma*, so we apply this *damma* to أَلِفٌ making it اُكْتُبُ. Then سُكُونٌ is given to the *last* letter making it: اُكْتُبْ (uktub) meaning: *write*.

8. And the فِعْلُ الأَمْرِ from يَفْتَحُ (where the third letter has *fatha*) and يَجْلِسُ (in which the third letter has *kasra*) is اِفْتَحْ and اِجْلِسْ respectively.

Because:

(a) the *second* letter is vowelless, so we introduce أَلِفٌ.

(b) the *third* letter has فَتْحَةٌ in يَفْتَحُ and كَسْرَةٌ in يَجْلِسُ, so in both cases we give *kasra* to this أَلِفٌ, and

(c) the *last* letter of فِعْلُ الأَمْرِ is given سُكُونٌ.

9. The conjugation of فِعْلُ الأَمْرِ has *six* moods which comprise of suffixes only:

(1) اُكْتُبْ: (masculine singular) <u>write</u>: *suffix*: NIL

(2) اُكْتُبَا: (masculine dual) <u>write</u>: *suffix*: أَلِفٌ

(3) اُكْتُبُوا: (masculine plural) <u>write</u>: *suffix*: وا

(4) اُكْتُبِي: (feminine singular) <u>write</u>: *suffix*: ي

(5) اُكْتُبَا: (feminine dual) <u>write</u>: *suffix*: أَلِفٌ

(6) اُكْتُبْنَ: (feminine plural) <u>write</u>: *suffix*: نَ

10. There are two *exceptional* imperatives: تَعَالَ (come!) and هَاتِ بَرِنْ (bring!) These two are exceptional. They occur only as فِعْلُ الأَمْرِ (imperative). They have *no* past or present tense. Therefore the grammarians call them اِسْمُ الْفِعْلِ *"ismul-fi'li"* meaning "noun of the verb" because they are basically nouns but Arabs use them as imperative verbs. Their conjugation runs as:

(Come!) تَعَالَ, تَعَالَيَا, تَعَالَوْا, تَعَالَيْ, تَعَالَيَا and تَعَالَيْنَ

54

(Bring! Fetch!) هَاتِينَ and هَاتِيَا, هَاتِي, هَاتُوا, هَاتِيَا, هَاتِ

11. The prefix أَلِفٌ in the imperative originally called هَمْزَةُ الْوَصْلِ (*hamzatul-wasli:* joining hamzah) is *not* pronounced if a vowelled consonant *precedes* it, e.g. وَاُقْرَأْ كِتَابَكَ (*waqra* and not: wa-iqra) meaning: *and read your book.*

12. The سُكُونٌ on the last letter of فِعْلُ الأَمْرِ: اقْرَأْ الدَّرْسَ is changed with *kasra* if it follows a noun with 'alif and laam' as in اِقْرَأ الـدَّرْسَ (*iqra-id-darsa* and not: *iqra ad-darsa*). Only *kasra* is allowed in such positions. It is applied in order to facilitate smooth pronunciation and avoid break in it.

13. Some 'imperative verbs' are:

(1)	اِقْرَأْ	: Read!	(from:	(قَرَأَ يَقْرَأُ
(2)	أُسْكُنْ	: Live!	(from:	(سَكَنَ يَسْكُنُ
(3)	اِسْمَعْ	: Hear!	(from:	(سَمِعَ يَسْمَعُ
(4)	اذْهَبْ	: Go!	(from:	(ذَهَبَ يَذْهَبُ
(5)	اِلْعَبْ	: Play!	(from:	(لَعِبَ يَلْعَبُ

EXERCISE

Grammatically analyse the following sentences:

(1) *Go* to your room and *read* your book.

اِذْهَبْ إِلَى غُرْفَتِكَ وَاَقْرَأْ كِتَابَكَ.

Idh-hab ilaa ghurfatika waqra kitaabaka.

(2) Majid, *sit* on your desk and *read* the new lesson.

يَا مَاجِدُ، اِجْلِسْ عَلَى مَكْتَبِكَ وَاَقْرَأِ الدَّرْسَ الْجَدِيدَ.

Yaa Maajidu, ijlis 'ala maktabika waqra id-darsal-jadiida.

(3) *Open* your note book and *write* a short essay.

اِفْتَحْ كُرَّاسَتَكَ وَاُكْتُبْ مَقَالَةً قَصِيرَةً.

55

Iftaḥ kurraasataka waktub maqaalatan qaṣiiratan.

(4) Fatima, *go* to the school in the morning and *play* in the garden in the evening.

يَا فَاطِمَةُ، اِذْهَبِي إِلَى الْمَدْرَسَةِ فِي الصَّبَاحِ وَٱلْعَبِي فِي الْحَدِيقَةِ فِي الْمَسَاءِ.

Yaa Faatimatu, idh-habii ilal-madrasati fiṣ-ṣabaaḥi wal'abii fil-ḥadiiqati fil-masaai.

(5) *Write* your name on the new notebook.

اُكْتُبِ اسْمَكَ عَلَى الكُرَّاسَةِ الجَدِيدَةِ.

Uktubis maka 'alal-kurraasatil-jadiidati.

GRAMMATICAL ANALYSIS

يَا مَاجِدُ، اِجْلِسْ عَلَى مَكْتَبِكَ وَ اَقْرَأُ الدَّرْسَ الْجَدِيدَ.

(8)	(7)	(6)	(5)	(4)	(3)	(2)	(1)
↓	↓	↓	↓	↓	↓	↓	↓
مَفْعُولٌ	فِعْلُ الأَمْرِ	حَرْفُ الأَمْرِ	حَرْفٌ	مَجْرُورٌ	حَرْفُ	الْمُنَادَى	حَرْفُ
↓	↓		عَطْفٍ	↓	جَرٍّ	↓	النِّدَاء
التَّشْكِيلُ:فَتْحَةٌ	وَالْفَاعِلُ:			كَ:		اَلْفَاعِلُ:	التَّشْكِيلُ:
↓	أَنْتَ			ضَمِيرٌ		أَنْتَ	ضَمَّةٌ
مَوْصُوفٌ				مُتَّصِلٌ			
↓							
صِفَةٌ							

---

1. يَا = is a word with which you '*call* someone'. It is called the '*vocative particle*' or حَرْفُ النِّدَاء (ḥarfun-nadaai).

2. مَاجِدُ = is the word coming *after* حَرْفُ النِّدَاء and it is called الْمُنَادَى (al-munaada). Its تَشْكِيلٌ is '*damma*' without nunation.

3. اِجْلِسْ = فِعْلُ الأَمْرِ is for *masculine singular*. It has a built-in أَنْتَ which is فَاعِلٌ.

4. عَلَى = is حَرْفُ جَرٍّ *a preposition.*

5. ضَمِيرٌ مُتَّصِلٌ = is مَجْرُورٌ. Its تَشْكِيلٌ is *kasra* and كَ is مَكْتَبِكَ (*possessive pronoun*) suffixed to it.

6. وَ = means 'and'. It is called *the 'conjunction'* or حَرْفُ العَطْفِ (*harful-'atfi*).

7. اِقْرَأْ = is the second فِعْلُ الأَمْرِ. Its فَاعِلٌ is أَنْتَ. With وَ before اِقْرَأْ and the *alif* being *hamzatul-wasli*, it is pronounced 'waqra' (وَاقْرَأْ).

8. الدَّرْسَ الْجَدِيدَ = is مَفْعُولٌ the تَشْكِيلٌ of which is *fatha*. And it is also مَوْصُوفٌ and صِفَةٌ. The صِفَةٌ *agrees* with the مَوْصُوفٌ in four respects:

   (a) it has the 'definite article' (أَلِفٌ وَلاَمٌ),

   (b) it is masculine,

   (c) it is singular and

   (d) it has *fatha*.

INSTRUCTIONS

As the making of correct فِعْلُ الأَمْرِ depends on your knowing the correct اَلْفِعْلُ الْمُضَارِعُ, keenly observe its *'second'* and *'third'* letter. In case something is less than totally clear, slowly re-read the lesson grasping one point at a time. And make a habit of grammatically analysing all the sentences in the exercise. It will make you conscious of the correct place of each and every word in a sentence.

فِعْلُ النَّهْي

The Negative Imperative Verb

EXAMPLE

Do not write on the blackboard. لاَ تَكْتُبْ عَلَى السَّبُّورَةِ.
↓
فِعْلُ النَّهْي

NEGATIVE
IMPERATIVE
VERB

---

1. The 'negative imperative verb' like *'don't go'* is called فِعْلُ النَّهْي *(fi'lun-nahyii)*.

2. This verb *prohibits* an action. The verb: *'go'* is فِعْلُ الأَمْرِ and *'don't go'* is: فِعْلُ النَّهْي.

3. فِعْلُ النَّهْي is derived from فِعْلُ الأَمْرِ.
   For example: from فِعْلُ الأَمْرِ : اُكْتُبْ, أَلِفٌ is *removed* and when in its place the prefix لاَ and تَ is brought, it becomes : لاَ تَكْتُبْ *(laa taktub)* meaning : *'Do not write'*.

5. In فِعْلُ النَّهْي too the *last* letter remains 'vowelless' (سَاكِنٌ).

6. The conjugation of فِعْلُ النَّهْي has *six* moods expressed by suffixes exactly like فِعْلُ الأَمْرِ :

   (1) لاَ تَكْتُبْ = (masculine singular) don't write: suffix: nil

   (2) لاَ تَكْتُبَا = (masculine dual) don't write: suffix: ا

   (3) لاَ تَكْتُبُوا = (masculine plural) don't write: suffix: وا

   (4) لاَ تَكْتُبِي = (feminine singular) don't write: suffix: ى

(5) لاَ تَكْتُبَا = (feminine dual) don't write: suffix: ا

(6) لاَ تَكْتُبْنَ = (feminine plural) don't write: suffix: نَ

7. <u>Some 'negative imperative verbs' are:</u>

(1) from : اِفْتَحْ (open) لاَ تَفْتَحْ (don't open).

(2) from : اِجْلِسْ (sit) لاَ تَجْلِسْ (don't sit).

(3) from : اِسْمَعْ (listen) لاَ تَسْمَعْ (don't listen).

(4) from : اِذْهَبْ (go) لاَ تَذْهَبْ (don't go).

(5) from : اِلْعَبْ (play) لاَ تَلْعَبْ (don't play).

EXERCISE

(1) *Don't open* the door.   لاَ تَفْتَحِ الْبَابَ.

Laa taftahil-baaba.

(2) *Don't play* in the street.   لاَ تَلْعَبْ فِي الشَّارِعِ.

Laa tal'ab fish-shaari'i.

(3) Su'aad, *don't go* to her house.   يَا سُعَادُ، لاَ تَذْهَبِي إِلَى بَيْتِهَا.

Yaa Su'aadu, laa tadh-habii ila baitihaa.

(4) Samiya, *don't sit* on that chair.

يَا سَامِيَةُ، لاَ تَجْلِسِي عَلَى ذَلِكَ الْكُرْسِيِّ.

Yaa Saamiyatu, laa tajlisii 'alaa dhaalikal kursiyyi.

(5) Ahmad, *don't read* my letter.   يَا أَحْمَدُ، لاَ تَقْرَأْ رِسَالَتِي.

Yaa Ahmadu, laa taqra risaalatii.

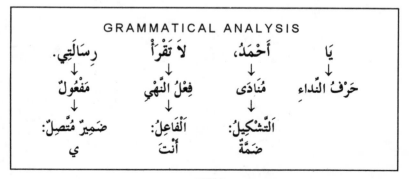

59

(1) يَا = is a 'vocative particle' or حَرْفُ النّدَاءِ (ḥarfun-nidaai).

(2) أَحْمَدُ = in this sentence is called اَلْمُنَادَى or *'the person being called'*. Its تَشْكِيلٌ is *damma without nunation*.

(3) لاَ تَقْرَأْ = is فِعْلُ النَّهْيِ for masculine singular. Its فَاعِلٌ is أَنْتَ. It is *implicit* and therefore it is *not* written.

(4) رسَالَتِي = is اَلْمَفْعُولُ and ي is ضَمِيرٌ مُتَّصِلٌ attached to it.

INSTRUCTIONS

1. Memorise the conjugation of فِعْلُ النَّهْيِ.
2. Grammatically analyse all the remaining sentences.

أَهَمُّ الْمُصْطَلَحَاتِ النَّحْوِيَّةِ

The Miscellany
Important Grammatical Terms

᠁

The following are some of the most important grammatical terms. As you have gained the knowledge of basic rules, now you should also be acquainted with the terms which are frequently used. Pay utmost attention to "the grammatical analysis."

1. اَلنَّكِرَةُ

An-nakiratu:
THE INDEFINITE NOUN

An indefinite noun like 'a pen' is called نَكِرَةٌ (*nakiratun*).

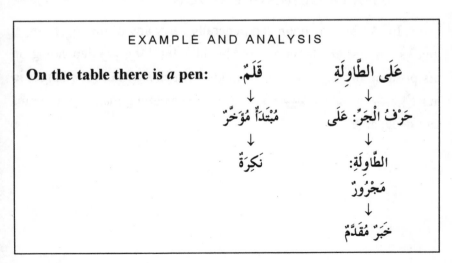

EXAMPLE AND ANALYSIS

On the table there is *a* pen:

قَلَمٌ.
↓
مُبْتَدَأٌ مُؤَخَّرٌ
↓
نَكِرَةٌ

عَلَى الطَّاوِلَةِ
↓
حَرْفُ الْجَرِّ: عَلَى
↓
الطَّاوِلَةِ:
مَجْرُورٌ
↓
خَبَرٌ مُقَدَّمٌ

---

2. اَلْمَعْرِفَةُ
Al-ma'rifatu:
THE DEFINITE NOUN

A 'definite noun' like '*the* book' is called مَعْرِفَةٌ *ma'rifatun*.

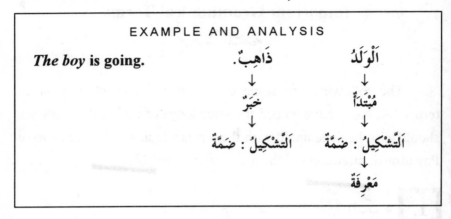

EXAMPLE AND ANALYSIS

The boy is going.

3. اَلْمُعْرَبُ
Al-mu'rabu:
THE DECLINABLE NOUN

In Arabic, a noun can generally carry any of the three vowel marks on its *last* letter as need be, like وَلَدٌ, وَلَدًا, وَلَدٍ depending on its position in a sentence. Thus a noun which *may accept* changes in its تَشْكِيلٌ is called اِسْمٌ مُعْرَبٌ. An overwhelming majority of nouns are declinable.

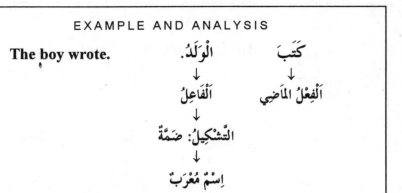

EXAMPLE AND ANALYSIS

The boy wrote. الْوَلَدُ.   كَتَبَ

↓   ↓

ٱلْفَاعِلُ   ٱلْفِعْلُ الْمَاضِي

↓

التَّشْكِيلُ: ضَمَّةٌ

↓

اِسْمٌ مُعْرَبٌ

4. ٱلْمَبْنِيُّ

Al-mabniyyu:

THE INDECLINABLE NOUN

A noun which has a fixed تَشْكِيلٌ on its *last* letter like : هُوَ
(with fixed *fatha*) or مِنْ (with fixed سُكُونٌ) is called ٱلْمَبْنِيُّ.

Such *'indeclinable nouns'* are *never* influenced by their
position in a sentence.

The noteworthy *indeclinable nouns* are (1) all the أَسْمَاءُ
الْإِشَارَةِ (demonstrative pronouns) like هَـٰذَا, هَـٰذِهِ, ذَلِكَ and تِلْكَ,
(2) ضَمَائِرُ (pronouns) like هُوَ, هِيَ, أَنْتَ, أَنْتِ, and أَنَا; ضَمَائِرُ مُتَّصِلَةٌ
(3) أَدَوَاتُ (possessive pronouns) like كِ, كَ, هَا, ه, and ي etc.
الْإِسْتِفْهَام (particles of interrogation) like هَلْ, مَتَى, أَيْنَ, كَيْفَ and مَاذَا
etc. (4) حُرُوفُ الْجَرِّ (prepositions) like فِي, إِلَى, عَلَى, بِ, etc.

63

EXAMPLE AND ANALYSIS

He is going to his office.

هُوَ	ذَاهِبٌ	إلَى	مَكْتَبِهِ.
(1)	(2)	(3)	(4)
↓	↓	↓	↓
مُبْتَدَأٌ	خَبَرٌ	حَرْفُ جَرٍّ	مَجْرُورٌ
↓	↓	↓	↓
اَلتَّشْكِيلُ	اَلتَّشْكِيلُ	مَبْنِيٌّ عَلَى	ضَمِيرٌ
ضَمَّة	ضَمَّة	السُّكُونِ	مُتَّصِلٌ
↓			
ضَمِيرٌ مُنْفَصِلٌ			
↓			
مَبْنِيٌّ عَلَى الفَتْحَةِ			

1. هُوَ : is *the subject* (اَلْمُبْتَدَأُ). Its vowel mark should be *damma*. But as it is a *'personal pronoun nominative'* (ضَمِيرٌ مُنْفَصِلٌ), it has a 'fixed vowel mark': *fatha* (مَبْنِيٌّ عَلَى الفَتْحَةِ).

2. ذَاهِبٌ : is *'the predicate'* (اَلْخَبَرُ). Its vowel mark is *damma*.

3. إلَىْ : is a *'preposition'*. It has a *'fixed vowel mark'*: *sukuun* (مَبْنِيٌّ عَلَى السُّكُونِ).

4. مَكْتَبِهِ : is *'a noun governed by a preposition'* (مَجْرُورٌ). Its vowel mark is *kasra*. And a *'personal pronoun possessive'* (ضَمِيرٌ مُتَّصِلٌ) is suffixed to it.

5. الْجُمْلَةُ الاسْمِيَّةُ

Al-jumlatul-ismiyyatu:

THE NOMINAL SENTENCE

64

A 'nominal sentence' or one beginning with a *noun* is called:
اَلْجُمْلَةُ الاِسْمِيَّةُ (al-jumlatul-ismiyyatu).

EXAMPLE AND ANALYSIS

The girl is going.

ذَاهِبَةٌ	اَلْبِنْتُ
(2)	(1)
↓	↓
اَلْخَبَرُ	اَلْمُبْتَدَأُ
↓	↓
التَّشْكِيلُ: ضَمَّةٌ	التَّشْكِيلُ: ضَمَّةٌ
	↓
	اِسْمٌ

---

1. اَلْبِنْتُ: It is the 'subject' (اَلْمُبْتَدَأُ). Its vowel mark is *damma*. اَلْبِنْتُ is a noun (اِسْمٌ), therefore this is a *nominal sentence* (جُمْلَةٌ اِسْمِيَّةٌ).

2. ذَاهِبَةٌ: It is the 'predicate' (اَلْخَبَرُ). Its vowel mark is *damma*. Both the subject and predicate agree with each other in being feminine.

---

6. | اَلْجُمْلَةُ الْفِعْلِيَّةُ

Al-jumlatul-fiʿliyyatu:
THE VERBAL SENTENCE

A 'verbal sentence' or one beginning with a *verb*, whether in مَاضٍ, مُضَارِعٌ, أَمْرٌ, or نَهْيٌ is called اَلْجُمْلَةُ الْفِعْلِيَّةُ.

> EXAMPLE AND ANALYSIS
>
> **The guard opened the gate.**
>
> اَلْبَابَ   اَلْحَارِسُ   فَتَحَ
>
> ↓   ↓   ↓
>
> اَلْمَفْعُولُ   اَلْفَاعِلُ   اَلْفِعْلُ الْمَاضِي
>
> ↓   ↓
>
> اَلتَّشْكِيلُ: فَتْحَةٌ   اَلتَّشْكِيلُ: ضَمَّةٌ

7. حُرُوفُ الْعَطْفِ

Huruuful-'Atfi:
THE CONJUNCTIONS

The following words in Arabic are called the *conjunctions* or حُرُوفُ الْعَطْفِ. They *do not* produce any change in the تَشْكِيلٌ of the next word. They are مَبْنِيٌّ i.e. 'indeclinable'.

(1) وَ = "and". It gives the sense of 'simultaneity' as in: ذَهَبَ مَاجِدٌ وَ خَالِدٌ (Majid *and* Khalid went).

(2) أَوْ = "or". It indicates 'choice', as in : اِقْرَأْ هذَا أَوْ ذَلِكَ (Read this *or* that).

(3) فَ = "then/so". It indicates 'coordination and immediate sequence' as in: جَاءَتْ زَيْنَبُ فَسُعَادُ (Zainab came *and then* Su'ad).

(4) ثُمَّ = "then". It indicates 'coordination and retarded sequence', as in: أَكَلَ الْمَرِيضُ الطَّعَامَ ثُمَّ شَرِبَ الدَّوَاءَ (The patient had (ate) the meal *then* took (drank) the medicine).

(5) أَمْ = "or" (only in questions) as in: أَهَذَا كِتَابُكَ أَمْ ذَلِكَ ؟ (Is this your book *or* that one?)

(6) بَلْ = "rather" or 'but' as in: مَا حَضَرَ الْمُدِيرُ بَلِ الْكَاتِبُ (The manager did not come, *rather* the clerk came).

(7) لَكِنْ = "but" as in: اَلسَّيَّارَةُ صَغِيرَةٌ وَ لَكِنِ الْحَافِلَةُ كِبِيرَةٌ (The car is small *but* the bus is big). Besides حَرْفُ الْعَطْفِ, it is also called حَرْفُ الْإِسْتِدْرَاكِ (harful-istidraaki).

(8) حَتَّى = "even". As in : فَرَّ الْجَيْشُ حَتَّى قَائِدُهُ (The army fled *even* its commander).

EXAMPLE AND ANALYSIS
The car is small but the bus is big.

اَلسَّيَّارَةُ	صَغِيرَةٌ	وَلَكِنِ	الْحَافِلَةُ	كَبِيرَةٌ.
(1)	(2)	(3)	(4)	(5)
↓	↓	↓	↓	↓
مُبْتَدَأٌ	خَبَرٌ	حَرْفُ عَطْفٍ	مُبْتَدَأٌ	خَبَرٌ
↓	↓	↓	↓	↓
مَعْرِفَةٌ اَلتَّشْكِيلُ: ضَمَّةٌ	اَلتَّشْكِيلُ: ضَمَّةٌ	حَرْفُ الْإِسْتِدْرَاكِ	مَعْرِفَةٌ	اَلتَّشْكِيلُ: ضَمَّةٌ
↓	↓	↓		↓
مُعْرَبٌ	مُؤَنَّثٌ	مَبْنِيٌّ عَلَى السُّكُونِ		مُؤَنَّثٌ

---

1. اَلسَّيَّارَةُ : is 'the subject' (اَلْمُبْتَدَأُ). It is 'definite' (مَعْرِفَةٌ). Its vowel mark (تَشْكِيلٌ) is *damma*. It is 'declinable' (مُعْرَبٌ), which means: it is a noun that has the capacity to accept either damma, fatha or *kasra,* as the need be.

2. صَغِيرَةٌ: is 'the predicate' (الْخَبَرُ). Its vowel mark is *damma*. It agrees with the subject in being feminine (مُؤَنَّثٌ). The symbol of its being feminine is 'round ة' called اَلتَّاءُالْمُدَوَّرَةُ *or* اَلتَّاءُالْمَرْبُوطَةُ

3. وَلَكِنْ : is a 'conjunction' (حَرْفُ عَطْفٍ). It is also called: حَرْفُ

67

الاسْـتِدْراكِ. Like other conjunctions, it does *not* cause any change in the next word. As we have already learnt, any word with its last letter without vowel (سَاكِنْ) as is the case with وَلَكِـنْ gets *kasra* in place of سُكُونْ if the word coming *after* it has the definite article اَلْ as in وَلَكِنِ الْحَافِلَةُ. This movement *kasra* prevents a break and facilitates flow in sound. Thus it is 'walaakinil-haafilatu' (and not *walaakin al-haafilatu*).

4. اَلْحَافِلَةُ : As the word preceding وَلَكِـنْ does *not* cause any change, الْحَافِلَـةُ remains another *subject* (اَلْمُبْتَدَأُ), the تَشْكِيلٌ of which is *damma*.

5. كَبِيرَةٌ : is the predicate (الْخَبَرُ). Its vowel mark is *damma*. And it agrees with the subject in being feminine (مُؤَنَّثٌ).

8. أَسْمَاءُ الإشَارَةِ
Asmaa-ul-ishaarati:
THE DEMONSTRATIVE PRONOUNS

In English this and that' are called '*the demonstrative pronouns*'. In Arabic, they are called أَسْمَاءُ الإشَارَةِ. For referring to masculine, they are هَذَا and ذَلِكَ, for feminine they are هَذِهِ and تِلْكَ. Unless you see the indefinite article 'a' as in this sentence: 'this is *a* book', هَذَا كِتَابٌ, keep اِسْمُ الإشَارَةِ prefixed to a noun with أَلِفٌ ولاَمٌ e.g. "this book: هَذَا الْكِتَابُ" or "this girl: هَذِهِ الْبِنْتُ".

Also note that in the example هَذَا الكِتَابُ — هَذَا is اِسْمُ الإشَارَةِ and الْكِتَابُ is الْمُشَارُ إلَيْهِ (the one pointed to).

68

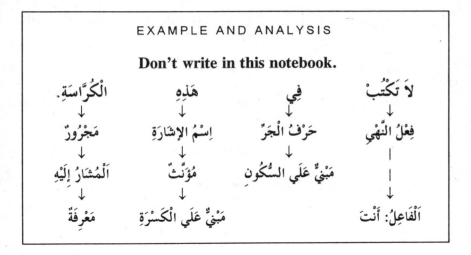

Don't write in this notebook.

الْكُرَّاسَةِ.	هَذِهِ	فِي	لَا تَكْتُبْ
↓	↓	↓	↓
مَجْرُورٌ	اِسْمُ الإِشَارَةِ	حَرْفُ الْجَرِّ	فِعْلُ النَّهْي
↓	↓	↓	|
اَلْمُشَارُ إِلَيْهِ	مُؤَنَّثٌ	مَبْنِيٌّ عَلَى السُّكُونِ	|
↓	↓		↓
مَعْرِفَةٌ	مَبْنِيٌّ عَلَى الْكَسْرَةِ		اَلْفَاعِلُ: أَنْتَ

9. اَلْفِعْلُ الثُّلَاثِيُّ الْمُجَرَّدُ

Al-fi'luth-thulaathil-mujarradu:

THE PRIMITIVE TRILITERAL VERB

The Primitive Triliteral Verb (PTV) or *'a verb having only three letters'* like كَتَبَ or فَتَحَ is called اَلْفِعْلُ الثُّلَاثِيُّ الْمُجَرَّدُ.

In Arabic, the verbs may have four, five and even six letters. Those verbs having more than three letters are called اَلْفِعْلُ الْمَزِيدُ فِيهِ (al-fi'lul-maziidu fiihi). In this book only the primitive triliteral verbs are discussed. The اَلْفِعْلُ الْمَزِيدُ فِيهِ will be discussed later.

We have already noticed that only the *second* letter of اَلْمَاضِي differs in التَّشْكِيلُ as *fatha* in كَتَبَ and *kasra* in سَمِعَ. And only the *third* letter of الْمُضَارِعُ differs in تَشْكِيل as *damma* on كُ in يَسْكُنُ, *fatha* on تَ in يَفْتَحُ, and *kasra* on لِ in يَجْلِسُ. So as in English where the Present Tense Verb 'go' becomes *went* or 'eat' becomes *'ate'* in past tense, the Primitive Triliteral Verb (PTV) too may take the following *six* forms:

1. **Category: A-U :** كَتَبَ يَكْتُبُ : Here the *second* letter of مَاضٍ has *fatha* vowel 'A', and the *third* letter of مُضَارِعٌ has *damma* (vowel 'U').

2. **Category: A-A :** فَتَحَ يَفْتَحُ : We call it A-A category because the *second* letter of مَاضٍ has *fatha* (vowel 'A'); and the *third* letter of مُضَارِعٌ too has fatha (vowel 'A').

3. **Category: A-I :** جَلَسَ يَجْلِسُ : We call it A-I category because the *second* letter of مَاضٍ has *fatha* (vowel 'A'); and the *third* letter of مُضَارِعٌ too has *kasra* (vowel 'I').

4. **Category: I-A :** سَمِعَ يَسْمَعُ : We call it I-A category because the *second* letter of مَاضٍ has *kasra* (vowel 'I'); and the *third* letter of مُضَارِعٌ has fatha (vowel 'A').

Note that over ninety percent of *triliteral verbs* belong to the above four A-U, A-A, A-I, I-A categories. The remaining ten percent verbs mostly belong to the following two categories:

5. **Category: U-U:** قَرُبَ يَقْرُبُ means: 'to go near' or 'to be near something'. We call it U-U category because the *second* letter of مَاضٍ has *damma* (vowel 'U'); and the *third* letter of مُضَارِعٌ too has *damma* (vowel 'U').

6. **Category: I-I :** حَسِبَ يَحْسِبُ : Very few Arabic verbs belong to this category. We call it the I-I category because the *second* letter of مَاضٍ has *kasra* (vowel 'I'); and the *third* letter of مُضَارِعٌ too has *kasra* (vowel 'I').

These six categories of اَلثُّلَاثِيُّ الْمُجَرَّدُ are not very important in themselves, they just introduce you to the forms which the past and present tense verb may take. As in English : *'sit'* is 'sat' in Past

70

Tense, 'go' is *'went'*, 'fix' is *'fixed'*, 'eat' is *'ate'*, and 'take' is *'took'*.

10. أَدَوَاتُ الاِسْتِفهَام

Adawaatul-istifhaami:

THE PARTICLES OF INTERROGATION

The following words are called أَدَوَاتُ الاِسْتِفهَام or the *particles of interrogation*:

(A) مَنْ ؟ = who?

(B) أَيْنَ ؟ = where?

(C) كَيْفَ؟ = how?

(D) مَا/مَاذَا ؟ = what?

(E) لِمَاذَا ؟ = why?

(F) مَتَى ؟ = when?

(G) أَيُّ، أَيَّةُ = which?

Except أَيُّ (ayyu) discussed in the next point, all the أَدَوَاتُ الاِسْتِفهَام are 'indeclinable' (مَبْنِيٌّ) and therefore their تَشْكِيلٌ *never* changes.

As you have already noticed the two interrogative particles هَلْ and أ have *no* meaning of their own. They are used to confirm or deny something. For example :

(1) هَلْ هُوَ قَادِمٌ ؟ : Is he coming ?

(2) هَلْ أَنْتَ سَعِيدٌ ؟ : Are you happy ?

(3) هَلْ أَنَا مُتَأَخِّرٌ ؟ : Am I late?

(4) أَ حَضَرْتَ أَمْسِ؟ : Did you come yesterday?

(5) هَلْ تَدْرُسُ ؟ : Do you study?

(6) هَلْ سَتَكْتُبُ ؟ : Will you write?

71

You can confirm or deny these questions by nodding your head in affirmation or shaking it in negative *unlike* the question asked with أَيْنَ as أَيْنَ الْكِتَابُ؟ (where is the book?) in which you have to use *specific words* to reply e.g.: الْكِتَابُ عَلَى الطَّاوِلَةِ (the book is over the table).

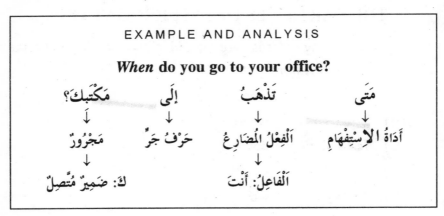

EXAMPLE AND ANALYSIS

When do you go to your office?

11. أَيُّ and أَيَّةُ
Ayyu and Ayyatu:
WHICH?

These two words mean 'which'. They too are *particles of interrogation* but with a difference. They appear only as مُضَاف. Since they are مُضَاف, they may accept any تَشْكِيل. The word coming *after* أَيُّ is مُضَاف إِلَيْهِ, the تَشْكِيل of which is كَسْرَة.

(a) أَيُّ should refer to *masculine* e.g.: أَيُّ كِتَابٍ (*which* book?) though it can *also* refer to *feminine* e.g. أَيُّ بِنْتٍ نَجَحَتْ؟ (*which* girl succeeded?).

(b) أَيَّةُ with its suffix of *round* ة can only refer to the *feminine* e.g. أَيَّةُ بِنْتٍ نَجَحَتْ؟ (*which* girl succeeded?).

72

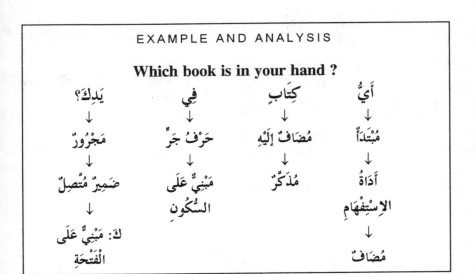

EXAMPLE AND ANALYSIS

Which book is in your hand ?

MORE ANALYSIS

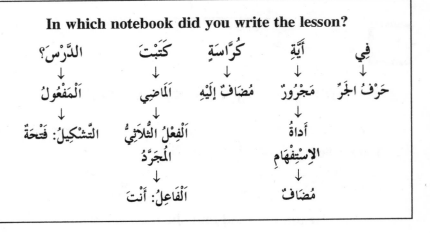

In which notebook did you write the lesson?

12.

jiddan:
VERY

For 'Very' as in 'very big', the word is جِدًّا (*jiddan*) and it is brought *after* the adjective. It stays as it is always irrespective of

73

masculine or feminine adjective. It is called تَوْكِيدُ الْخَبَرِ (tawkiid'ul-khabari).

مَفْعُولٌ مُطْلَقٌ لِلْمُبَالَغَةِ (jiddan is also called مَفْعُولٌ مُطْلَقٌ لِلْمُبَالَغَةِ or in short جِدَّاً لِلْمُبَالَغَةِ meaning: jiddan for intensification).

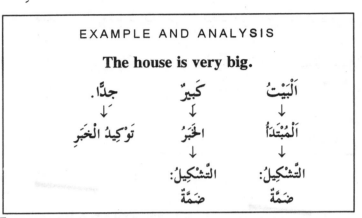

EXAMPLE AND ANALYSIS

The house is very big.

جِدَّا.	كَبِيرٌ	اَلْبَيْتُ
↓	↓	↓
تَوْكِيدُ الْخَبَرِ	الْخَبَرُ	اَلْمُبْتَدَأُ
	↓	↓
	التَّشْكِيلُ:	التَّشْكِيلُ:
	ضَمَّةً	ضَمَّةً

13. حُرُوفُ النَّفْي

Huruufun-nafyi:

THE PARTICLES OF NEGATION

مَا before الْفِعْلُ الْمَاضِي as in قَرَأْتُ مَا and لاَ before الْمُضَارِعُ as in لاَ أَقْرَأُ are called حُرُوفُ النَّفْي 'the particles of negation'.

EXAMPLE AND ANALYSIS

He *did not* read and she *does not* read.

تَقْرَأُ.	لاَ	وَ	قَرَأَ	مَا
↓	↓	↓	↓	↓
اَلْفِعْلُ الْمُضَارِعُ	حَرْفُ النَّفْي	حَرْفُ الْعَطْفِ	اَلْفِعْلُ الْمَاضِي	حَرْفُ النَّفْي
↓		↓	↓	↓
وَالْفَاعِلُ:		مَبْنِيٌّ عَلَى	اَلْفِعْلُ الثُّلاَثِيُّ الْمُجَرَّدُ	مَبْنِيٌّ عَلَى
هِيَ		الفَتْحَةِ	↓	السُّكُونِ
			اَلْفَاعِلُ: هُوَ	

74

14. اَلْمُنَادَى and حُرُوفُ النِّدَاء

Huruufun-nidaa'i and al-munaada:
THE VOCATIVE PARTICLES

(a) يَا the *vocative particle* in يَا مَاجِدُ (O' Majid) is called the حَرْفُ النِّدَاء (*harfun-nidaa'i*). We use *O'* the vocation particle to call someone. In English it is hardly used but in Arabic it is used quite often.

(b) The noun *after* حَرْفُ النِّدَاء like مَاجِدُ is called مُنَادَى (*munaada*: i.e. the *person being called*).

(c) If this مُنَادَى consists of a *single* word, its تَشْكِيلٌ is ضَمَّةٌ *without nunation* as in يَا مَاجِدُ.

(d) If the مُنَادَى is formed by مُضَافٌ وَمُضَافٌ إِلَيْهِ as in يَا عَبْدَ اللهِ (O' Abdullah: slave *of* God) or يَا طَالِبَ الْفَصْلِ (O' student of the class), it is given فَتْحَةٌ (*fatha*).

(e) Two oft-used *vocative particles* are (1) أَيُّهَا (ayyuhaa) and يَا أَيُّهَا (*yaa-ayyuhaa*) for 'masculine *definite noun*' like: أَيُّهَا الْوَلَدُ or يَا أَيُّهَا الْوَلَدُ اقْرَأْ! (O' boy, read!) (2) أَيَّتُهَا (ayyatuhaa) and يَا أَيَّتُهَا (yaa-ayyatuha) for 'feminine *definite* noun' as: يَا أَيَّتُهَا الْبِنْتُ اِقْرَأِي (O' girl, read!).

These two do *not* accept proper names as مُنَادَى. In other words, يَا أَيُّهَا أَحْمَدُ is *incorrect*.

EXAMPLE AND ANALYSIS

O' Abdullah, read your lesson.

حَرْفُ النِّدَاءِ ← يَا

الْمُنَادَى ← عَبْدَ اللهِ

مُضَافٌ

ومُضَافٌ إِلَيْهِ ←

اَلتَّشْكِيلُ: فَتْحَةٌ

فِعْلُ الأَمْرِ ← اِقْرَأْ

لِلْمُذَكَّرِ   ضَمِيرٌ مُتَّصِلٌ: كَ

وَالْفَاعِلُ: أَنْتَ   مَبْنِيٌّ عَلَى الفَتْحَةِ

مَفْعُولٌ ← دَرْسَكَ.

15. حُرُوفُ الإِسْتِقْبَال

Huruuful-istiqbaali:

THE PARTICLES OF FUTURE

The *'particles of future'* like سَ and سَوْفَ are حُرُوفُ الإِسْتِقْبَالِ. In English the word 'will' is used to make a *future* tense verb. In Arabic, either سَ or سَوْفَ is prefixed to اَلْفِعْلُ الْمُضَارِعُ to turn it into a future tense verb. As in: He *will* go: سَيَذْهَبُ or سَوْفَ يَذْهَبُ.

Note that سَ is joined to the verb and is *not* written separately e.g. سَيَذْهَبُ.

76

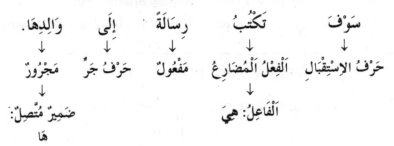

EXAMPLE AND ANALYSIS

She will write a letter to her father.

وَالِدِهَا.	إِلَى	رِسَالَةً	تَكْتُبُ	سَوْفَ
↓	↓	↓	↓	↓
مَجْرُورٌ	حَرْفُ جَرٍّ	مَفْعُولٌ	اَلْفِعْلُ اَلْمُضَارِعُ	حَرْفُ الْاِسْتِقْبَالِ
↓			↓	
ضَمِيرٌ مُتَّصِلٌ: هَا			اَلْفَاعِلُ: هِيَ	

---

16. أَدَاةُ التَّعْرِيفِ

Adaatut-taʻriifi:

THE DEFINITE ARTICLE

As you already know the definite article in Arabic is اَلْ and it is called أَدَاةُ التَّعْرِيفِ or لَاَمُ التَّعْرِيفِ. Any noun like وَلَدٌ *loses* its nunation when اَلْ is prefixed to make it definite: اَلْوَلَدُ. There are three oft-used categories of nouns which are considered definite *without* أَلِفٌ ولَاَمٌ, They are:

(1) *Proper Nouns:* For example: زَيْنَبُ, رَاشِدٌ, مُحَمَّدٌ and etc. No *alif laam* is prefixed to them. But as these are *definite*, the adjective (صِفَةٌ) will carry 'the definite article' e.g.

زَيْنَبُ الصَّغِيرَةُ قَادِمَةٌ. = (The) little Zainab is coming.

(2) *Nouns with possessive pronouns:* e.g. كِتَابُهُ or بَيْتِي are *definite* without *alif laam* and therefore their adjectives will carry 'the definite article'. For example: بَيْتِي الْجَدِيدُ جَيِّدٌ = *My new house* is good.

(3) *Nouns in construct state* (مُضَافٌ) with the *definite*: e.g. كُلِّيَّةُ كِتَابُ سُعَادَ or أَخِي are 'definite' without 'alif laam' because

77

كُلِّيَة and كِتَابُ both are *related to definite persons* (أَخِي and سُعَادُ). This relation makes them *'definite'* too. In case صِفَة is brought, it must carry 'the definite article'. For example: كُلِّيَة أَخِي الْقَدِيمَة بَعِيدَة = *The old* college of my brother is far away.

EXAMPLE AND ANALYSIS

The old college of my brother is far away.

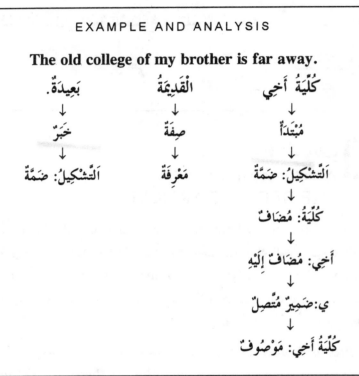

For 'also' as in "read that book also", the word is أَيْضًا (*aidan*). It stays *as it is* irrespective of masculine or feminine words. It is called أيضاً لِلتَّوْكِيدِ (aidan lit-tawkiidi) *'aidan' for emphasis.*

Read that book also.

اِقْرَأْ ← ذَلِكَ الْكِتَابَ ← أَيْضًا .

فِعْلُ الأَمْرِ ← مَفْعُولٌ ← لِلتَّوْكِيدِ

اَلْفَاعِلُ: أَنْتَ ← اَلتَّشْكِيلُ: فَتْحَةٌ

اِسْمُ الإِشَارَةِ : ذَلِكَ

اَلْكِتَابَ: اَلْمُشَارُ إِلَيْهِ

---

18. اَلْمَمْنُوعُ مِنَ الصَّرْفِ

Almamnuu'u minas sarfi:

THE DIPTOTE

The following categories of nouns and adjectives are called *diptotes* or اَلْمَمْنُوعُ مِنَ الصَّرْفِ because the Arabs, since time immemorial, do *not* give them *kasra* nor *tanwiin*. In case of kasra, they are given فَتْحَةٌ without تَنْوِينٌ. However, if such nouns and adjectives are definite with 'al', they can carry kasra.

(1) Most feminine proper names: Like: سُعَادُ، زَيْنَبُ، فَاطِمَةُ e.g. He went with Fatima. ذَهَبَ مَعَ فَاطِمَةَ (no *kasra* or *tanwiin* on Fatima).

(2) Arabicized foreign names: بَاكِسْتَان، إِيرَان، نِيُويُورك e.g. He went to Iran. ذَهَبَ إِلَى إِيرَانَ (no kasra or tanwiin on *Iran*).

(3) Adjectives denoting colours : like :

Red	أَحْمَرُ (masc.)	حَمْرَاءُ (fem.)	
Green	أَخْضَرُ (masc.)	خَضْرَاءُ (fem.)	

79

White	أَبْيَضُ (masc.)	بَيْضَاءُ (fem.)	
Blue	أَزْرَقُ (masc.)	زَرْقَاءُ (fem.)	

EXAMPLE AND ANALYSIS

Farida goes to her office in a red car.

تَذْهَبُ فَرِيدَةُ إِلَى مَكْتَبِهَا فِي سَيَّارَةٍ حَمْرَاءَ.

↓ ↓ ↓ ↓ ↓ ↓ ↓

اَلْفِعْلُ الْمُضَارِعُ   اَلْفَاعِلُ   حَرْفُ جَرٍّ   مَجْرُورٌ   حَرْفُ جَرٍّ   مَجْرُورٌ   صِفَةٌ

↓ ↓ ↓ ↓ ↓ ↓ ↓

اَلْفِعْلُ   اِسْمُ   مَبْنِيٌّ   ضَمِيرٌ   نَكِرَةٌ   مَمْنُوعٌ

الثُّلَاثِيُّ   امْرَأَةٍ   عَلَى   مُتَّصِلٌ: هَا   ↓   مِنَ الصَّرْفِ

الْمُجَرَّدُ   ↓   السُّكُون   مَوْصُوفٌ   ↓

مَمْنُوعٌ   نَكِرَةٌ

مِنَ الصَّرْفِ   ↓

اَلتَّشْكِيلُ: فَتْحَةٌ

Example of definite:

Farida goes to her office in *the* red car.

تَذْهَبُ فَرِيدَةُ إِلَى مَكْتَبِهَا فِي السَّيَّارَةِ الْحَمْرَاءِ.

19. اَلْفِعْلُ اللَّازِمُ

Al-fi'lul-laazimu:
THE INTRANSITIVE VERB

The *'intransitive verb'* whose action is confined to the *doer* like: to go: ذَهَبَ يَذْهَبُ or to sit: جَلَسَ يَجْلِسُ is called اَلْفِعْلُ الْفَاعِلُ اللَّازِمُ. Such verb *cannot* have an object or مَفْعُولٌ.

80

Hamid went to his college.

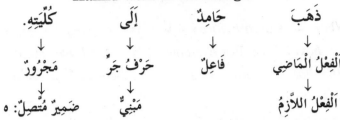

ذَهَبَ	حَامِدٌ	إِلَى	كُلِّيَّتِهِ.
↓	↓	↓	↓
اَلْفِعْلُ الْمَاضِي	فَاعِلٌ	حَرْفُ جَرٍّ	مَجْرُورٌ
↓		↓	↓
اَلْفِعْلُ اللَّازِمُ		مَبْنِيٌّ	ضَمِيرٌ مُتَّصِلٌ: ه

20. اَلْفِعْلُ الْمُتَعَدِّي

Al-fi'lul-muta'addii:
THE TRANSITIVE VERB

The *'transitive verb'* in which the action of the verb goes right upto the 'object' like 'to open' فَتَحَ يَفْتَحُ and 'to read' قَرَأَ يَقْرَأُ is called اَلْفِعْلُ الْمُتَعَدِّي. Such a verb has the capacity to have فَاعِلٌ as well as مَفْعُولٌ (unlike: ذَهَبَ).

I heard the voice of his father, so I opened the door for him.

سَمِعْتُ	صَوْتَ	وَالِدِهِ	فَفَتَحْتُ	الْبَابَ	لَهُ.
↓	↓	↓	↓	↓	↓
اَلْمَاضِي	مَفْعُولٌ	مُضَافٌ إِلَيْهِ	فَ:	مَفْعُولٌ	حَرْفُ الْجَرِّ
↓	↓	↓	حَرْفُ الْعَطْفِ	↓	↓
اَلْفِعْلُ الثُّلَاثِيُّ	مُضَافٌ	ضَمِيرٌ	↓	اَلتَّشْكِيلُ:	مَجْرُورٌ
الْمُجَرَّدُ		مُتَّصِلٌ: ه	اَلْفِعْلُ الْمَاضِي	فَتْحَةٌ	↓
↓			↓		ضَمِيرٌ
اَلْفِعْلُ الْمُتَعَدِّي			اَلْفِعْلُ الْمُتَعَدِّي		مُتَّصِلٌ: هُ
↓			↓		
اَلْفَاعِلُ: أَنَا			اَلْفَاعِلُ: أَنَا		

81

21. قَدْ

Qad:

(a) When قَدْ is used *before* اَلْفِعْلُ الْمَاضِي, it gives the sense of *'has'* or *'have'* done. For example: قَدْ أَكَلْتُ (I *have* eaten). قَدْ كَتَبَتْ (She *has* written). Here قَـدْ is called حَرْفُ التَّوْكِيـدِ (*harfut-tawkiidi*).

(b) When قَـدْ is used *before* اَلْفِعْلُ الْمُضَارِعُ, it indicates the incompleteness or tentativeness of the action generally conveyed by *may* or *perhaps* in English.

For example: قَـدْ تَرْجِعُ (She *may* return or *perhaps* she will return.) Here it is called قَدْ لِلتَّقْلِيلِ (qad lit-taqliili).

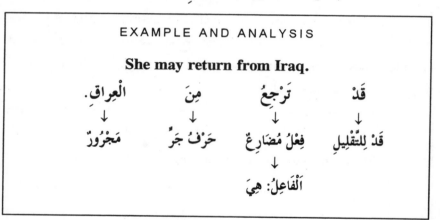

```
EXAMPLE AND ANALYSIS

She may return from Iraq.

الْعِرَاقِ.        مِنَ        تَرْجِعُ              قَدْ
   ↓            ↓           ↓                ↓
مَجْرُورٌ      حَرْفُ جَرٌّ   فِعْلُ مُضَارِعٌ    قَدْ لِلتَّقْلِيلِ
                              ↓
                        اَلْفَاعِلُ: هِيَ
```

22. نَعَمْ and لاَ

Na'am and Laa:

THE PARTICLES OF REPLY

The words نَعَمْ (yes) and لاَ (no) are called (*huruuful-jawaabi*) or 'particles of reply'.

Did you read the newspaper? Yes, I read it.

هَلْ   قَرَأْتَ   الْجَرِيدَةَ؟   نَعَمْ،   قَرَأْتُهَا.
↓   ↓   ↓   ↓   ↓

أَدَاةُ   اَلْفِعْلُ الْمَاضِي   الْمَفْعُولُ   حَرْفُ الْجَوَابِ   اَلْفِعْلُ الْمَاضِي
الاسْتِفْهَام
↓   ↓

وَالْفَاعِلُ: أَنْتَ   وَالْفَاعِلُ: أَنَا
↓
الْمَفْعُولُ:
ضَمِيرٌ مُتَّصِلٌ: هَا

When لَا comes *before* a verb, it is called حَرْفُ النَّفْي or 'particle of negation' as in لاَ يَقْرَأُ الدَّرْسَ بَعْدَ الغَدَاء (I do *not* read the lesson after lunch).

I do *not* read the lesson after lunch.

لَا   أَقْرَأُ   الدَّرْسَ   بَعْدَ   الْغَدَاءِ.
↓   ↓   ↓   ↓   ↓

حَرْفُ النَّفْي   اَلْفِعْلُ الْمُضَارِعُ   الْمَفْعُولُ   حَرْفُ جَرٍّ   مَجْرُورٌ
↓   ↓   ↓

وَالْفَاعِلُ:   اَلتَّشْكِيلُ:   اَلتَّشْكِيلُ:
أَنَا   فَتْحَةٌ   كَسْرَةٌ

23. الأَسْمَاءُ الْخَمْسَةُ

Al-asmaa'ul khamsatu:

THE FIVE NOUNS

الأَسْمَاءُ الْخَمْسَةُ means 'The five nouns'. They are:

(1) أَخٌ (akhun)   = a brother.

(2) أَبٌ (abun)   = a father.

(3) حَمٌ (hamun)   = a father-in-law.

(4) فَمٌ (famun)   = a mouth.

(5) ذو (dhuu)   = an owner or possessor (always followed by a noun).

These *five nouns* are regarded exclusive and separate from the rest because:

(a) if (1) أَخٌ, (2) أَبٌ and (3) حَمٌ are مُضَافٌ their *damma* becomes أَخَا as واو as in أَخٌ in : ذَهَبَ أَخُو مَاجِدٍ. Their *fatha* becomes أَلِفٌ as in أَخٍ in: ذَهَبْتُ مَعَ. Their *kasra* becomes ى as in أَخٍ in :رَأَيْتُ أَخَا مَاجِدٍ. أَخِي مَاجِدٍ.

(b) These *five nouns* are exclusive because if (4) فَمٌ is مُضَافٌ it altogether changes its shape and becomes: فُو in case of *damma* as in: فُوالأَسَدِ مَفْتُوحٌ = The *mouth* of the lion is open (الْمُبْتَدَأُ:). (التَّشكِيلُ: ضَمَّةٌ).

فَا in case of *fatha* as in: فَتَحَ الأَسَدُ فَاهُ = The lion opened its mouth (الْمَفْعُولُ: التَّشكِيلُ: فَتْحَةٌ).

فِي in case of *kasra* as in: وَضَعَ الطَّبِيبُ الدَّوَاءَ في في الْمَرِيضِ = The doctor put the medicine in the *mouth* of the patient. (الْمَجْرُورُ: التَّشكِيلُ: كَسْرَةٌ).

(c) These five nouns are exclusive because ذو meaning "owner or possesser" never comes *alone*. Instead a *noun* follows it as مُضَافٌ إِلَيْهِ. Together they act as a صِفَةٌ.

Example with *damma*

ذو مَال = rich (owner of wealth or money)

ذو عِلْمٍ = learned (possesser of knowledge)

ذُو عَقْلٍ = wise (possesser of wisdom or intelligence)

With *fatha* they are: ذَا عَقْلٍ and ذَا عِلْمٍ، ذَا مَالٍ .

With *kasra* they are: ذِي عَقْلٍ and ذِي عِلْمٍ، ذِي مَالٍ .

(d) The *feminine* for ذو, ذَا and ذِي is ذَاتُ, ذَاتَ andذَاتِ as in:

ذَاتُ مَالٍ   (wealthy)

ذَاتَ عِلْمٍ   (learned) and

ذَاتِ عَقْلٍ   (wise).

(e) Remember that فِي and فَا , فُو have become archaic and they are no more in everyday use. Nowadays the word فَمٌ is used with normal case endings, e.g.

فَمُ الْفِيلِ كَبِيرٌ (The *mouth* of the elephant is big) or

فَتَحَ الطَّبِيبُ فَمَ الْمَرِيضِ (The doctor opened the *mouth* of the patient). ·

EXAMPLE AND ANALYSIS

The doctor put the medicine in the mouth of the patient.

وَضَعَ	الطَّبِيبُ	الدَّوَاءَ	فِي	فِي	الْمَرِيضِ.
↓	↓	↓	↓	↓	↓
اَلْفِعْلُ	اَلْفَاعِلُ	اَلْمَفْعُولُ	حَرْفُ الْجَرِّ	أَحَدُ	مُضَافٌ إِلَيْهِ
اَلْمَاضِي	↓	↓		الأَسْمَاءِ الْخَمْسَةِ	
	اَلتَّشْكِيلُ:	اَلتَّشْكِيلُ:		↓	
	ضَمَّةٌ	فَتْحَةٌ		مَجْرُورٌ	
				↓	
				مُضَافٌ	

---

24. اَلْمُؤَنَّثُ السَّمَاعِيُّ

Al-mu'annathu as-samaa'iyyu:

FEMININE BY USAGE

You already know that generally all those words which end in round ة called اَلتَّاءُ الْمَرْبُوطَةُ (at-taa'ul-marbuutatu) are feminine. And those without this round ة are masculine.

In Arabic there are certain nouns which apparently *do not* have any symbol of being feminine like round ة (as: الشَّمْسُ = the sun) but still they are regarded by the Arabs as *feminine*. The Arabs have always " heard " these words being used as feminine and thus they are called مُؤَنَّثٌ سَمَاعِيٌّ or *feminine by usage*.

Much in use among such nouns are:

(1)	اَلْأَرْضُ (the earth)	(5)	اَلْحَرْبُ (the war)
(2)	اَلْكَأْسُ (the cup)	(6)	اَلنَّارُ (the fire)
(3)	اَلْخَمْرُ (the wine)	(7)	اَلرِّيحُ (the wind)
(4)	اَلدَّارُ (the house)	(8)	اَلشَّمْسُ (the sun)

Besides these, most parts of the body which are in *pairs* are regarded مُؤَنَّثٌ سَمَاعِيٌّ. They are :

(1)	اَلْيَدُ (the hand)	(5)	اَلْأُذُنُ (the ear)
(2)	الْإِصْبَعُ (the finger)	(6)	الذِّرَاعُ (the arm)
(3)	اَلرِّجْلُ (the leg)	(7)	اَلْعَيْنُ (the eye)
(4)	اَلْقَدَمُ (the foot)	(8)	اَلْكَفُّ (the palm)

The sun rises in the morning.

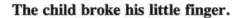

الصَّبَاح.	فِي	الشَّمْسُ	تَطْلُعُ
↓	↓	↓	↓
مَجْرُورٌ	حَرْفُ الْجَرِّ	اَلْفَاعِلُ	اَلْمُضَارِعُ
↓		↓	↓
التَّشْكِيلُ: كَسْرَةٌ		مُؤَنَّثٌ سَمَاعِيٌّ	اَلْفِعْلُ اللاَّزِم
			↓
			مُؤَنَّثٌ

ANOTHER EXAMPLE AND ANALYSIS:

The child broke his little finger.

الصَّغِيرَةَ.	إِصْبَعَهُ	الطِّفْلُ	كَسَرَ
↓	↓	↓	↓
صِفَةٌ	اَلْمَفْعُولُ	اَلْفَاعِلُ	اَلْفِعْلُ
↓	↓	↓	الثُّلاثِيُّ
مُؤَنَّثٌ	التَّشْكِيلُ: فَتْحَةٌ	التَّشْكِيلُ: ضَمَّةٌ	المُجَرَّدُ
↓	↓		↓
مَعْرِفَةٌ	مَوْصُوفٌ		اَلْفِعْلُ الْمَاضِي

25. عِنْدَ

'inda:
TO HAVE

(a) The word *has* as in " Majid *has* a book" is   expressed .by عِنْدَ.
For example: عِنْدَ مَاجِدٍ كِتَابٌ .

(b) عِنْدَ is مُضَافٌ, therefore the word after it is مُضَافٌ إِلَيْهِ, the
تَشْكِيلٌ of which is كَسْرَةٌ .e.g "Majid has a book": عِنْدَ مَاجِدٍ

87

عِنْدَ فَاطِمَةَ سَيَّارَةٌ :kitab or " Fatima has a car" : كِتَابٌ.

(c) ضَمِيرٌ مُتَّصِلٌ is suffixed to عِنْدَ for he *has* or she *has* etc.

For example:

He has	:	عِنْدَهُ
She has	:	عِنْدَهَا
You (m.) have	:	عِنْدَكَ
You (f.) have	:	عِنْدَكِ
I have	:	عِنْدِي

(d) This combination عِنْدَهُ or عِنْدَ مَاجِدٍ is *'definite'* thus it is generally regarded as خَبَرٌ مُقَدَّمٌ, and as "a book" is *indefinite*, it is regarded as مُبْتَدَأٌ مُؤَخَّرٌ.

EXAMPLE AND ANALYSIS

I have a bicycle and Fatima has a car.

سَيَّارَةٌ.	فَاطِمَةَ	عِنْدَ	وَ	دَرَّاجَةٌ	عِنْدِي
↓	↓	↓	↓	↓	↓
مُبْتَدَأٌ	مُضَافٌ إِلَيْهِ	خَبَرٌ مُقَدَّمٌ	حَرْفُ الْعَطْفِ	مُبْتَدَأٌ مُؤَخَّرٌ	خَبَرٌ مُقَدَّمٌ
مُؤَخَّرٌ	↓	↓		↓	↓
↓	اِسْمُ اِمْرَأَةٍ	مُضَافٌ		نَكِرَةٌ	عِنْدَ: مُضَافٌ
نَكِرَةٌ	↓	↓			↓
	مَمْنُوعٌ	مَبْنِيٌّ عَلَى			ضَمِيرٌ مُتَّصِلٌ: ي
	مِنَ الصَّرْفِ	الْفَتْحَةِ			↓
					مُضَافٌ إِلَيْهِ

---

26. هَمْزَةُ الْوَصْلِ

Hamzatul-wasli:

THE JOINING HAMZA

(1) The symbol ‿ on أ as in إِلَى ٱلْبَيْتِ or مِنَ ٱلْبَيْتِ denotes هَمْزَةُ الْوَصْلِ (*hamzatul-wasli*).

(2) The *alif* of 'the definite article' is called هَمْزَةُ الْوَصْلِ. It is *not* pronounced when it is *preceded* by a word e.g. إِلَى ٱلْبَيْتِ (ilal-baiti).

(3) In إِلَى ٱلْبَيْتِ the sound of the preposition *'ila'* is joined to the لْ of الْبَيْتِ e.g. *ila'l-baiti*. Do *not* pronounce it: *ila-al-baiti*.

(4) Besides the definite article, the other هَمْزَةُ ٱلْوَصْلِ is the prefix أَلِفٌ in the triliteral imperative verb: فِعْلُ الْأَمْرِ. وَٱكْتُبْ is: *waktub* (and write) and وَٱجْلِسْ is: *wajlis* (and sit).

(5) Some nouns too have هَمْزَةُ ٱلْوَصْلِ:

    (1) اِبْنٌ (a son)   (3) اِبْنَةٌ (a daughter)

    (2) اِسْمٌ (a name)   (4) اِمْرَأَةٌ (a woman)

---

27. الْمَصْدَرُ

Al-masdaru:
THE INFINITIVE

The 'verbal noun' or 'infinitive' is called الْمَصْدَرُ (al-masdaru). In English, the 'infinitive' or 'verbal noun' of the verb: to go is: *the going*. Go, Went and Gone are used only as verbs. But الْمَصْدَرُ: 'the going' can be used like any noun as مُبْتَدَأٌ, مُضَافٌ, فَاعِلٌ or مَوْصُوفٌ, مُضَافٌ إِلَيْهِ etc. It my carry nunation or the definite article like an ordinary noun.

As there is *no fixed rule* to turn a verb into a مَصْدَرٌ, it has to be learnt separately as part of the vocabulary. The student, from now onwards, must ask the teacher for the مَصْدَرٌ of each verb.

Some 'verbal nouns' are:

(1) From ذَهَبَ يَذْهَبُ it is: اَلذَّهَابُ = the going e.g.

The *going* to the college by bus is tiresome.

اَلذَّهَابُ إِلَى الْكُلِّيَّةِ بِالْبَاصِ مُتْعِبٌ.

89

(2) From كَتَبَ يَكْتُبُ it is: اَلْكِتَابَةُ = the writing e.g.

The *writing* on the blackboard is clear.

اَلْكِتَابَةُ عَلَى السَّبُّورَةِ وَاضِحَةٌ.

(3) From قَرَأَ يَقْرَأُ it is: اَلْقِرَاءَةُ = the reading.

The *reading* of this book is enjoyable.

قِرَاءَةُ هَذَا الْكِتَابِ مُمْتِعَةٌ.

EXAMPLE AND ANALYSIS

The *reading* of that book is enjoyable.

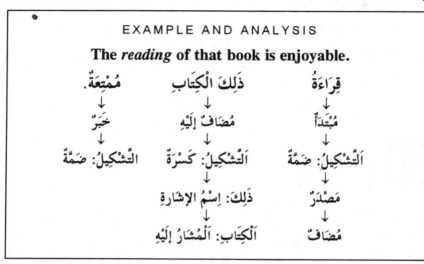

MORE ANALYSIS

The going to the college by bus is tiresome.

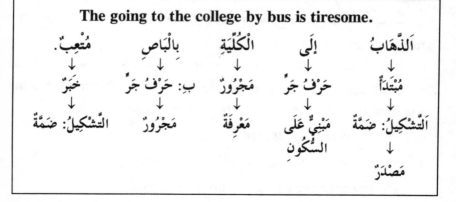

90

28. اَلأَلِفُ المَقْصُورَةُ

Al-alif ul-maqsuuratu:

THE MINIATURE ALIF

The miniature أَلِفٌ placed on ى as ىٰ in سَلْمىٰ is called اَلأَلِفُ المَقْصُورَةُ.

A noun having اَلأَلِفُ المَقْصُورَةُ does *not* undergo any change in تَشْكِيلٌ. For example:

1. *Salma* went to her office:

ذَهَبَتْ سَلْمىٰ إِلَى مَكْتَبِهَا. (فَاعِلٌ: اَلتَّشْكِيلُ: ضَمَّةٌ)

2. I saw *Lubna* in the hospital:

رَأَيْتُ لُبْنىٰ فِي الْمُسْتَشْفىٰ. (مَفْعُولٌ: اَلتَّشْكِيلُ: فَتْحَةٌ)

3. I had breakfast with *Huda* at her home:

أَكَلْتُ الْفَطُورَ مَعَ هُدىٰ فِي بَيْتِهَا. (مَجْرُورٌ: اَلتَّشْكِيلُ: كَسْرَةٌ)

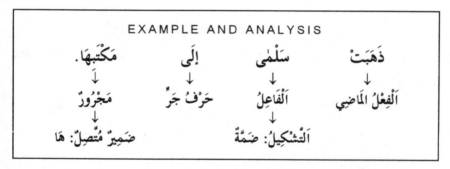

29. اَلْوَقْتُ

Al-Waqtu:

THE TIME

(1) In Arabic, the time *at 1 O'clock* is expressed in *two* words as صِفَةٌ and مَوْصُوفٌ:

فِى السَّاعَةِ الْوَاحِدَةِ	:	at 1 O'clock
فِى السَّاعَةِ الثَّانِيَةِ	:	at 2 O'clock
فِى السَّاعَةِ الثَّالِثَةِ	:	at 3 O'clock
فِى السَّاعَةِ الرَّابِعَةِ	:	at 4 O'clock
فِى السَّاعَةِ الْخَامِسَةِ	:	at 5 O'clock
فِى السَّاعَةِ السَّادِسَةِ	:	at 6 O'clock
فِى السَّاعَةِ السَّابِعَةِ	:	at 7 O'clock
فِى السَّاعَةِ الثَّامِنَةِ	:	at 8 O'clock
فِى السَّاعَةِ التَّاسِعَةِ	:	at 9 O'clock
فِى السَّاعَةِ الْعَاشِرَةِ	:	at 10 O'clock
فِى السَّاعَةِ الْحَادِيَةَ عَشْرَةَ	:	at 11 O'clock
فِى السَّاعَةِ الثَّانِيَةَ عَشْرَةَ	:	at 12 O'clock

(2) فِى is for *'at'*, بَعْدَ is for *'after'* and قَبْلَ is for *'before'*.

(3) Days of the week are expressed in two words as مُضَافٌ and مُضَافٌ إِلَيْهِ :

يَوْمَ الأَحَدِ	:	Sunday	يَوْمَ الْخَمِيسِ	:	Thursday
يَوْمَ الاِثْنَيْنِ	:	Monday	يَوْمَ الْجُمْعَةِ	:	Friday
يَوْمَ الثُّلاَثَاءِ	:	Tuesday	يَوْمَ السَّبْتِ	:	Saturday
يَوْمَ الأَرْبِعَاءِ	:	Wednesday			

EXAMPLE AND ANALYSIS

The manager returned at 1 O'clock on Friday.

رَجَعَ الْمُدِيرُ فِي السَّاعَةِ الوَاحِدَةِ يَوْمَ الْجُمْعَةِ.

اَلْفِعْلُ الْمَاضِي فَاعِلٌ حَرْفُ جَرٍّ مَجْرُورٌ مُضَافٌ مُضَافٌ إِلَيْهِ

اَلتَّشْكِيلُ: ضَمَّةٌ اَلْمَوْصُوفُ و الصِّفَةُ اَلتَّشْكِيلُ: فَتْحَةٌ ظَرْفُ الزَّمَان اَلتَّشْكِيلُ: كَسْرَةٌ

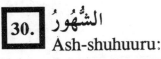

30. الشُّهُورُ
Ash-shuhuuru:
THE MONTHS

The *months* of the year are called شُهُورٌ (shuhuurun). The singular is: شَهْرٌ (shahrun): a month.

(1) In column 1, are the names used in Egypt and Sudan. They accept only *damma* and *fatha* without nunation. In case of *kasra*, they are given *fatha*. In other words they are مَمْنُوعٌ مِنَ الصَّرْفِ or diptotes.

(2) In column 2, are the names used in the Eastern Arab world. When combined they become صِفَةٌ and مَوْصُوفٌ.

(3) In column 3, are the months of the Muslim (lunar) year. When combined, these too are صِفَةٌ and مَوْصُوفٌ. They do not follow the sequence of the Christian calendar.

	COLUMN : 1	COLUMN : 2	COLUMN : 3
1. January	يَنَايِرُ	1. كَانُونُ الثَّانِى	مُحَرَّمُ

93

2.	February	فَبَرايِرُ	شُبَاطُ	2.	صَفَرُ
3.	March	مَارِسُ	آذَارُ	3.	الرَّبِيعُ الأَوَّلُ
4.	April	أَبْرِيلُ	نِيسَانُ	4.	الرَّبِيعُ الثَّانِي
5.	May	مَايُو	أَيَّارُ	5.	جُمَادَى الأُولَى
6.	June	يُونِيُو	حَزِيرَانُ	6.	جُمَادَى الآخِرَةُ
7.	July	يُولِيُو	تَمُّوزُ	7.	رَجَبُ
8.	August	أُغُسْطُسُ	آبُ	8.	شَعْبَانُ
9.	September	سِبْتَمْبِرُ	أَيْلُولُ	9.	رَمَضَانُ
10.	October	أُكْتُوبِرُ	تِشْرِينُ الأَوَّلُ	10.	شَوَّالُ
11.	November	نُوفِمْبِرُ	تِشْرِينُ الثَّانِي	11.	ذُوالْقَعْدَةِ
12.	December	دِيسِمْبِرُ	كَانُونُ الأَوَّلُ	12.	ذُوالحِجَّةِ

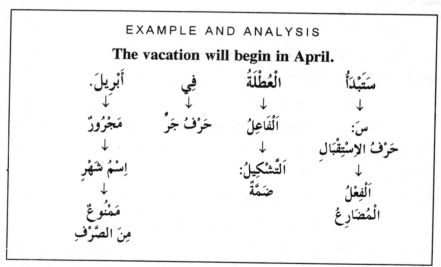

EXAMPLE AND ANALYSIS

The vacation will begin in April.

INSTRUCTIONS

Start by memorizing and using the names in column 1.

الفِعْلُ الْمُعْتَلّ

The Weak Verb

EXAMPLES

(a) قَالَ يَقُولُ (to say)   (e) جَرَي يَجْري (to run)

(b) بَاعَ يَبِيعُ (to sell)   (f) لَقِيَ يَلْقَى (to meet)

(c) نَامَ يَنامُ (to sleep)   (g) وَجَدَ يَجِدُ (to find)

(d) دَعَا يَدْعُو (to call)   (h) وَقَى يَقِي (to protect)

---

1. Observe the مَاض and its very different مُضَارِع in each of the eight kinds of verbs written above.

2. In Arabic, there are three *"weak letters"* or حُرُوفُ العِلّةِ. They are يَاء, أَلِف and وَاو.

3. A verb like كَتَبَ is called a *"strong verb"* or اَلْفِعْلُ الصَّحِيحُ because none of its three letters is a "weak letter" (حَرْفُ عِلّةٍ).

4. Any verb which has either و or ا or ي as its first, second or third letter is called a 'weak verb' or اَلْفِعْلُ الْمُعْتَلُ. For example: قَالَ يَقُولُ (to say) has أَلِفٌ in مَاض and وَاو in مُضَارِع.

5. These 'weak letters' are generally considered to be سَاكِنٌ or *'vowelless'*. Thus in the prepositions فِي, إِلَىْ and عَلَىْ, we find that the ي is 'vowelless'.

6. You should expect a few changes in the conjugations of verbs which either have وَاو or أَلِف or يَاء.

7. The main reason for such 'changes' is that in Arabic, no

95

اِجْتِمَاعُ السَّاكِنَيْن or *"coming together of two vowelless letters"* is ever allowed.

8. And whenever two vowelless letters come together, the 'weak one' from the two is *dropped*.

9. The oft-used 'weak verbs' which have some changes in their conjugations may take the following *eight forms*.

10. In these eight forms, observe that:

(a) in: قَالَ يَقُولُ (to say) the أَلِف in the *centre* of اَلْمَاضِي has become و in اَلْمُضَارِعُ: يَقُولُ.

(b) in: بَاعَ يَبِيعُ (to sell) the أَلِف in the *centre* of اَلْمَاضِي has become ي in اَلْمُضَارِعُ.

(c) in: نَامَ يَنَامُ (to sleep) the أَلِف in *centre* of اَلْمَاضِي is اَلِف in اَلْمُضَارِعُ too.

(d) in: دَعَا يَدْعُو (to call) the أَلِف in *end* of اَلْمَاضِي has become و in اَلْمُضَارِعُ.

(e) in: جَرَى يَجْرِي (to run) the ي in the *end* of اَلْمَاضِي maintains same position in اَلْمُضَارِعُ.

(f) in: لَقِيَ يَلْقَى (to meet) the ي in the *end* of اَلْمَاضِي maintains same position in اَلْمُضَارِعُ.

(g) in: وَجَدَ يَجِدُ (to find) the و in the *beginning* of اَلْمَاضِي is dropped in اَلْمُضَارِعُ.

(h) in: وَقَى يَقِي (to protect) the و in the *beginning* of اَلْمَاضِي is dropped in اَلْمُضَارِعُ.

11. Among other things you observe here that (a) قَالَ (b) بَاعَ and (c) نَامَ all have أَلِفٌ in the middle but their مُضَارِعٌ is different, thus together they make different *forms*.

12. Such *eight forms* of 'the weak verbs' are being presented and discussed under eight sections in the following pages.

96

13. In each section, besides four conjugations of مَاضٍ, مُضَارِعٌ, أَمْرٌ and نَهْـيٌ you will also find a list of oft-used verbs identified on the *form* discussed there. First memorize the conjugations, then practise other verbs on its pattern.

14. The *eight sections* are as following:

SECTION: 12-A: The Form : قَالَ يَقُولُ ('*12*' in 12-A *indicates* the lesson number)

SECTION : 12-B : The Form : بَاعَ يَبِيعُ

SECTION : 12-C : The Form : نَامَ يَنَامُ

SECTION : 12-D : The Form : دَعَا يَدْعُو

SECTION : 12-E : The Form : جَرَى يَجْرِى

SECTION : 12-F : The Form : لَقِيَ يَلْقَى

SECTION : 12-G : The Form : وَجَدَ يَجِدُ

SECTION : 12-H : The Form : وَقَى يَقِى

15. After describing the مَاضٍ, مُضَارِعٌ, أَمْرٌ and نَهْـيٌ of each Form separately, an effort has been made to explain as to how a particular mood in the conjugation undergoes a change so that one understands it thoroughly rather than be forced to accept it at its face value leaving many questions unanswered and doubts uncleared. But in a few cases where these changes appear slightly illogical or where they have simply been sanctioned by common usage, their explanation has been withheld.

THE FORM : قَالَ يَقُولُ (to say)

1. In the conjugation of قَالَ يَقُولُ , you will observe that the *prefixes* and *suffixes* of مَاضٍ, مُضَارِعٌ, أَمْرٌ and نَهْيٌ are similar to those discussed earlier.

2. But wherever اِجْتِمَاعُ السَّاكِنَيْن or *"coming together of two vowelless letters"* happens, changes occur.

3. The Conjugations are:

اَلنَّهْيُ	اَلْأَمْرُ	اَلْمُضَارِعُ	اَلْمَاضِي
1. لا تَقُلْ	1. قُلْ	1. يَقُولُ	1. قَالَ
2. لا تَقُولاَ	2. قُولاَ	2. يَقُولاَن	2. قَالاَ
3. لا تَقُولُوا	3. قُولُوا	3. يَقُولُونَ	3. قَالُوا
4. لا تَقُولِي	4. قُولِي	4. تَقُولُ	4. قَالَتْ
5. لا تَقُولاَ	5. قُولاَ	5. تَقُولاَن	5. قَالَتَا
6. لا تَقُلْنَ	6. قُلْنَ	6. يَقُلْنَ	6. قُلْنَ
		7. تَقُولُ	7. قُلْتَ
		8. تَقُولاَن	8. قُلْتُمَا
		9. تَقُولُونَ	9. قُلْتُمْ
		10. تَقُولِينَ	10. قُلْتِ
		11. تَقُولاَن	11. قُلْتُمَا
		12. تَقُلْنَ	12. قُلْتُنَّ
		13. أَقُولُ	13. قُلْتُ
		14. نَقُولُ	14. قُلْنَا

4. **Explanation of the 12-A changes in اَلْفِعْلُ اَلْمَاضِي : قَالَ**

Since no اِجْتِمَاعُ السَّاكِنَيْن *(coming together of two vowelless*

98

letters) happened from number 1 to number 5, no change occurred. But at no. 6 قُلْنَ , you find that (a) أَلِفٌ is *missing* and (b) a *damma* seems to have come from nowhere. The reason for these two changes is that اِجْتِمَاعُ السَّاكِنَيْن has taken place which required *dropping* of أَلِفٌ the 'weak letter', in the following manner : قَالَ يَقُوْلُ was actually قَوَلَ يَقْوُلُ. As this original form قَوَلَ يَقْوُلُ was not smooth on the Arab tongue, they changed it to قَالَ يَقُوْلُ. *This original shape remains hidden until such a change is to be explained.* To explain the change in no. 6 قُلْنَ, we go back to قَوَلَ, the original. Thus we find that قُلْنَ was قَوَلْنَ. According to rule, when *weak letters* like و or ي are *'movable'* (مُتَحَرِّكٌ) in a word and are preceded by a *letter with fatha* (as قَ was قَوَلْنَ), the و or ي are changed into alif , thus قَوَلْنَ becomes قَالْنَ. In it two letters viz. أَلِفٌ and ل are سَاكِنٌ (quiescent), so *alif* the weak letter is dropped and قَالْنَ becomes قَلْنَ. To show that the dropped letter is واو, vowel *damma*, which corresponds to و, is given to ق thus قَوَلْنَ becomes قُلْنَ.

Since similar اِجْتِمَاعُ السَّاكِنَيْن took place at every level from No. 6 onwards, you notice similar changes : (a) أَلِفٌ is missing and (b) ق has *damma* ضَمَّةٌ right upto no. 14.

5. **Explanation of the 12-A changes in** اَلْفِعْلُ اَلْمُضَارِعُ : يَقُوْلُ

When you observe this conjugation, you find no اِجْتِمَاعُ السَّاكِنَيْن except at number 6 يَقُلْنَ and number 12 تَقُلْنَ. The third letter و is somehow missing in these two cases. If you retain this و you find that تَقُوْلْنَ is تَقُلْنَ and يَقُوْلْنَ is يَقُلْنَ. As اِجْتِمَاعُ السَّاكِنَيْن takes place here you drop the weak letter واو . The weak letter واو like أَلِف and ي are regarded سَاكِنٌ or 'quiescent'.

6. **Explanation of the 12-A changes in فِعْلُ الأَمْرِ : قُلْ**

   (a) As you recall, فِعْلُ الأَمْرِ is made from اَلْفِعْلُ الْمُضَارِعُ. If the *second* letter of اَلْفِعْلُ الْمُضَارِعُ is سَاكِنٌ (vowelless), a prefix أَلِفٌ is introduced. If it is *not* سَاكِنٌ then nothing is introduced, making it قُوْلْ. The *last* letter in فِعْلُ الأَمْرِ is given سُكُوْنٌ thus : يَقُوْلُ becomes قُوْلْ. Since اِجْتِمَاعُ السَّاكِنَيْنِ is taking place, the *weak letter* واو is *dropped*. Thus قُوْلُ becomes: قُلْ.

   (b) From 2 to 5 that is in قُوْلاَ، قُوْلُوا، قُوْلِي and قُوْلاَ the واو is *not* dropped as it is *not* causing اِجْتِمَاعُ السَّاكِنَيْنِ.

   (c) But no.6, قُلْنَ, with واو is قُوْلْنَ from which اِجْتِمَاعُ السَّاكِنَيْنِ necessitates the *dropping of the weak letter* وَاو making it قُلْنَ.

   (d) Thus : قُلْ - قُوْلاَ - قُوْلُوا - قُوْلِي - قُوْلاَ and قُلْنَ.

7. **Explanation of 12-A changes in فِعْلُ النَّهْيِ : لاَ تَقُلْ**

   (a) As you can recall, فِعْلُ النَّهْيِ is derived from فِعْلُ الأَمْرِ.

   (b) Except at no. 1 and no. 6 , there are *no* changes here.

   (c) لاَ تَقُلْ was actually لاَ تَقُوْلْ in which you can find اِجْتِمَاعُ السَّاكِنَيْنِ. The weak letter واو is dropped making it لاَ تَقُلْ.

   (d) From 2 to 5 that is in : لاَ تَقُوْلاَ، لاَ تَقُوْلُوا، لاَ تَقُوْلِي and لاَ تَقُوْلاَ, the واو is *not* dropped because it is *not causing* اِجْتِمَاعُ السَّاكِنَيْنِ.

   (e) But no. 6: لاَ تَقُلْنَ is basically لاَ تَقُوْلْنَ in which اِجْتِمَاعُ السَّاكِنَيْنِ necessitates the dropping of the weak letter واو.

8. Commonly used Weak Verbs similar to قَالَ يَقُوْلُ of SECTION: 12-A are :

	اَلنَّهْيُ	اَلْأَمْرُ	اَلْمُضَارِعُ	اَلْمَاضِي	
(1)	لَا تَزُرْ	زُرْ	يَزُورُ	زَارَ	= to visit
(2)	لَا تَقُمْ	قُمْ	يَقُومُ	قَامَ	= to stand up
(3)	لَا تَصُمْ	صُمْ	يَصُومُ	صَامَ	= to keep fast
(4)	لَا تَسُقْ	سُقْ	يَسُوقُ	سَاقَ	= to drive
(5)	لَا تَسُدْ	سُدْ	يَسُودُ	سَادَ	= to head, to prevail
(6)	لَا تَدُرْ	دُرْ	يَدُورُ	دَارَ	= to circle, to revolve
(7)	لَا تَفُزْ	فُزْ	يَفُوزُ	فَازَ	= to be successful, to win
(8)	لَا تَطُفْ	طُفْ	يَطُوفُ	طَافَ	= to walk around, to roam
(9)	لَا تَتُبْ	تُبْ	يَتُوبُ	تَابَ	= to repent
(10)	لَا تَعُدْ	عُدْ	يَعُودُ	عَادَ	= to return

9. Learn to identify each weak verb in مَاض and its مُضَارِعٌ with *sections*. Memorize all the conjugations before proceeding to Section 12-B.

INSTRUCTIONS

Experience has shown that due to omissions and changes, the Weak Verb remains a point of weakness even at higher levels of learning. It is found to be very useful if the grammar teacher writes down all the four conjugations of each section on the blackboard and makes the students practise in chorus.

SECTION : 12-B

THE FORM : بَاعَ يَبِيعُ

1. Note that بَاعَ is similar to قَالَ but its مُضَارِعٌ has ي which puts it in a separate category.

2. As you have already seen, the basic prefixes and suffixes of مَاضٍ, مُضَارِعٌ, أَمْرٌ and نَهْيٌ are exactly the same as those of a 'strong' verb such as كَتَبَ etc.

3. The changes occur only due to اِجْتِمَاعُ السَّاكِنَيْنِ (coming together of two vowelless letters).

4. The conjugations for بَاعَ يَبِيعُ (to sell) are:

اَلنَّهْيُ	اَلْأَمْرُ	اَلْمُضَارِعُ	اَلْمَاضِي
1. لَا تَبِعْ	1. بِعْ	1. يَبِيعُ	1. بَاعَ
2. لَا تَبِيعَا	2. بِيعَا	2. يَبِيعَان	2. بَاعَا
3. لَا تَبِيعُوا	3. بِيعُوا	3. يَبِيعُونَ	3. بَاعُوا
4. لَا تَبِيعِي	4. بِيعِي	4. تَبِيعُ	4. بَاعَتْ
5. لَا تَبِيعَا	5. بِيعَا	5. تَبِيعَان	5. بَاعَتَا
6. لَا تَبِعْنَ	6. بِعْنَ	6. يَبِعْنَ	6. بِعْنَ
		7. تَبِيعُ	7. بِعْتَ
		8. تَبِيعَان	8. بِعْتُمَا
		9. تَبِيعُونَ	9. بِعْتُمْ
		10. تَبِيعِينَ	10. بِعْتِ
		11. تَبِيعَان	11. بِعْتُمَا
		12. تَبِعْنَ	12. بِعْتُنَّ
		13. أَبِيعُ	13. بِعْتُ
		14. نَبِيعُ	14. بِعْنَا

5. In these conjugations of بَاعَ يَبِيعُ, you can observe changes

102

occurring exactly on the pattern of the previous section 12-A
قَالَ يَقُولُ. In other words:

(a) in مَاضٍ : a change occurs at no. 6 بِعْنَ and goes on till no. 14.

(b) in مُضَارِعٌ : changes occur only at no. 6 يَبِعْنَ and no. 12 تَبِعْنَ.

(c) in أَمْرٌ : changes occur only at no. 1 بِعْ and no. 6 بِعْنَ.

(d) in نَهْيٌ changes occur only twice at no. 1 لَا تَبِعْ and no. 6 لَا تَبِعْنَ.

6. Although a thorough discussion of how and why these changes came about is being given below, it is better if you learn just to accept them and master the conjugations given in Point 4 through keen observation and repetitions.

7. **Explanation of the 12-B changes in** بَاعَ : اَلْفِعْلُ اَلْمَاضِي

(The 12 in 12-B indicates the lesson number)

From number 1 to number 5, *no* اِجْتِمَاعُ السَّاكِنَيْن takes place and thus there is *no* change. But at no. 6 بِعْنَ you find that (a) أَلِفٌ is missing and (b) a *kasra* seems to have come from nowhere. The reason for these changes is to be found in اِجْتِمَاعُ السَّاكِنَيْن which requires dropping of 'the weak letter' in the following manner: بِعْنَ from بَيَعَ was يَبَعْنَ. Here a weak letter ي is movable (مُتَحَرِّكٌ) and it is preceded by a letter (بَ) which has *fatha*. According to grammarians, the weak letter ي is changed into أَلِفٌ which is سَاكِنٌ (quiescent) turning بَيَعْنَ into بَاعْنَ. Because of 'coming together of two vowelless letters' in بَاعْنَ, the weak letter أَلِفٌ is *dropped* making it بَعْنَ. To show that the dropped letter was actually ي, a vowel *kasra* which corresponds to ي is given to بِ. Thus بَيَعْنَ becomes بِعْنَ.

103

Since similar اِجْتِمَاعُ السَّاكِنَيْن took place at every stage from number 6 onwards, therefore you notice similar changes: (a) أَلِفٌ is missing and (b) بِ has *kasra* right upto number 14 of the conjugation.

8. **Explanation of the 12-B changes in** يَبِيعُ : اَلْفِعْلُ الْمُضَارِعُ

Here changes took place only at two places. Firstly, at number 6 which was يَبِيعْنَ As اِجْتِمَاعُ السَّاكِنَيْن occurred, ي the weak letter preceding ع was dropped making it يَبِعْنَ. The second change was at no. 12 تَبِيعْنَ where the *coming together of two vowelless letters* ي and عْ necessitated the *dropping* of the weak letter يْ making it: يَبِعْنَ.

9. **Explanation of the 12-B changes in** بِعْ : فِعْلُ الأَمْر

(a) The فِعْلٌ مُضَارِعٌ: يَبِيْعُ is instrumental in the formation of فِعْلُ الأَمْر. If the second letter is *vowelless* only then the فِعْلُ الأَمْر is prefixed with أَلِفٌ otherwise nothing is prefixed to it. Thus يَبِيعُ becomes بِيعُ. When the last letter of فِعْلُ الأَمْر is made vowelless, بِيعُ becomes بِيْعْ. Here we drop the weak letter ي due to اِجْتِمَاعُ السَّاكِنَيْن making it بِعْ.

(b) From 2 to 5, that is: in بِيعَا , بِيعُوا , بِيعِي and بِيعَا, the weaker letter ي is *not* dropped because it is *not* causing اِجْتِمَاعُ السَّاكِنَيْن.

(c) But number 6 بِيْعْنَ with ي unremoved is بِيعْنَ from which اِجْتِمَاعُ السَّاكِنَيْن necessitated the omission of the weak letter ي making it : بِعْنَ.

(d) Thus : بِعْ - بِيعَا - بِيعُوا - بِيعِي - بِيعَا and بِعْنَ = *sell*.

10. **Explanation of the 12-B changes in** فِعْلُ النَّهِي: لَا تَبِعْ.

(a) As only لاَ and تَ with *fatha* is prefixed to turn a فِعْلُ الأَمْر

into فِعْلُ النَّهْيِ, the changes taking place in فِعْلُ الأَمْرِ also occur in فِعْلُ النَّهْيِ.

(b) لا تَبِعْ was actually لا تَبِيْعْ in which you can find the اِجْتِمَاعُ السَّاكِنَيْنِ. The weak letter ي is omitted making it: لا تَبِعْ.

(c) From 2 to 5 that is in : لا تَبِيعِي - لا تَبِيعُوا - لا تَبِيعَا and لا تَبِيعَا, the weak letter ي is *not* dropped because it is *not* causing اِجْتِمَاعُ السَّاكِنَيْنِ

(d) The number 6 is اِجْتِمَاعُ السَّاكِنَيْنِ in which لا تَبِيْعْنَ necessitated the dropping of ي making it لا تَبِعْنَ.

11. Some commonly used verbs on the pattern of بَاعَ - يَبِيعُ are:

(1) غَابَ يَغِيبُ (to be absent)
(2) مَالَ يَمِيلُ (to incline)
(3) صَادَ يَصِيدُ (to hunt)
(4) جَاءَ يَجِيءُ (to come)
(5) سَارَ يَسِيرُ (to move, to get going)
(6) عَاشَ يَعِيشُ (to live)
(7) طَارَ يَطِيرُ (to fly)
(8) سَالَ يَسِيلُ (to flow)
(9) صَاحَ يَصِيحُ (to shout)
(10) طَابَ يَطِيبُ (to be good, pleasant)

EXERCISE

FOR SECTION 12-A قَالَ يَقُولُ AND SECTION 12-B بَاعَ يَبِيعُ

Grammatically analyse the following sentences :

1. When does your father return from his office?

مَتَى يَعُودُ وَالِدُكَ مِنْ مَكْتَبِهِ؟

2. Her brother won the first prize in the match.

فَازَ أَخُوهَا بِالْجَائِزَةِ الأُولَى فِي الْمُبَارَاةِ.

3. The earth circles around the sun.

تَدُورُ الأَرْضُ حَوْلَ الشَّمْسِ.

4. The lady teacher said: "Do not be absent from the class."

قَالَتِ الْمُدَرِّسَةُ : "لَا تَغِبْ عَنِ الْفَصْلِ".

5. The aeroplane flies in the sky.

تَطِيرُ الطَّائِرَةُ فِي السَّمَاءِ.

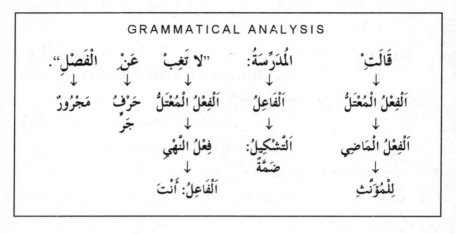

INSTRUCTIONS

Recite the conjugations of each weak verb used in these sentences.

THE FORM: نَامَ يَنَامُ (To sleep)

1. The مَاض here is نَامَ and مُضَارِعْ is يَنَامُ. Both have اَلِفْ. Note that this present tense verb is different from يَقُولُ and يَبِيعُ, the two forms discussed earlier.

2. The Conjugations of this Form are as follows:

اَلنَّهْيُ	اَلأَمْرُ	اَلْمُضَارِعُ	اَلْمَاضِي
1. لا تَنَمْ	1. نَمْ	1. يَنَامُ	1. نَامَ
2. لا تَنَامَا	2. نَامَا	2. يَنَامَان	2. نَامَا
3. لا تَنَامُوا	3. نَامُوا	3. يَنَامُونَ	3. نَامُوا
4. لا تَنَامِي	4. نَامِي	4. تَنَامُ	4. نَامَت
5. لا تَنَامَا	5. نَامَا	5. تَنَامَان	5. نَامَتَا
6. لا تَنَمْنَ	6. نَمْنَ	6. يَنَمْنَ	6. نِمْنَ
		7. تَنَامُ	7. نِمْتَ
		8. تَنَامَان	8. نِمْتُمَا
		9. تَنَامُونَ	9. نِمْتُمْ
		10. تَنَامِينَ	10. نِمْتِ
		11. تَنَامَان	11. نِمْتُمَا
		12. تَنَمْنَ	12. نِمْتُنَّ
		13. أَنَامُ	13. نِمْتُ
		14. نَنَامُ	14. نِمْنَا

3. **Explanation of the changes in 12-C: اَلْفِعْلُ اَلْمَاضِي : نَامَ.**

   You have already noticed in the مَاض of Section A and B, that the change occurs at no. 6. In نَامَ too the change takes place at no. 6 and as in the conjugations of قَالَ and بَاعَ they go on till no. 14.

4. **Explanation of the changes in 12-C: اَلْفِعْلُ الْمُضَارِعُ : يَنامُ.**

In the conjugation of اَلْفِعْلُ الْمُضَارِعُ, you notice two changes: one at no. 6 يَنمْنَ and the other one at no. 12 تَنمْنَ. In both these cases the أَلِفٌ is missing. The no. 6 was يَنَامْنَ and since اِجْتِمَاعُ السَّاكِنَيْنِ took place, the *weak letter* أَلِفٌ was *dropped* making it يَنمْنَ. The no. 12 تَنمْنَ was تَنَامْنَ. Here too اِجْتِمَاعُ السَّاكِنَيْنِ caused the dropping of the *weak letter* اَلِفٌ making it تَنمْنَ.

5. **Explanation of the changes in 12-C: فِعْلُ الأَمْرِ : نَمْ.**

    While observing the changes in فِعْلُ الأَمْرِ you should by now be able to detect اِجْتِمَاعُ السَّاكِنَيْنِ

    (a) The *imperative verb* is derived from اَلْفِعْلُ الْمُضَارِعُ : يَنَامُ.

    (b) If the second letter is سَاكِنٌ *only then* the فِعْلُ الأَمْرِ is prefixed with أَلِفٌ otherwise *not*.

    (c) Thus يَنَامُ becomes نَامُ. When سُكُونٌ is given to the last letter نَامُ, it becomes نَامْ. "The coming together of two vowelless letters" necessitates *dropping* of the *weak letter* أَلِفٌ. Hence : نَمْ (sleep!).

    (d) In nos. 2 to 5 نَامَا - نَامِي - نَامُوا - نَامَا no اِجْتِمَاعُ السَّاكِنَيْنِ takes place, therefore there are *no* changes.

    (e) In no. 6 نَمْنَ, you find that the أَلِفٌ is missing. It was originally نَامْنَ. The coming together of two vowelless letters أَلِفٌ and مْ necessitated the *dropping* of حَرْفُ الْعِلَّةِ: أَلِفٌ making it: نَمْنَ.

6. **Explanation of the changes in 12-C: فِعْلُ النَّهي: لا تَنَمْ.**

    The *negative imperative* depends on فِعْلُ الأَمْرِ for its form and changes. The prefix لا and تَ with *fatha* is given to *all* the six moods.

    (a) لا تَنَمْ becomes نَمْ from لا تَنَامْ.

108

(b) Nos. 2 to 5: لَا تَنَامَـا ـ لَا تَنَامُوا ـ لَاتَنَامِي and لَا تَنَامَا do not undergo any changes as *no* اِجْتِمَاعُ السَّاكِنَيْن occurs.

(c) Number 6 لَا تَنَمْنَ was لَا تَنَـأْمْنَ. The *coming together of two vowelless letters* necessitated the *dropping* of the weak letter أَلِفٌ.

7. Commonly used verbs on the pattern of 12-C are:

(1) خَافَ يَخَافُ: to fear, to be afraid.

(2) نَالَ يَنَالُ: to gain, to achieve.

(3) هَابَ يَهَابُ: to be afraid, to be awed.

INSTRUCTIONS

Memorize the conjugations of these verbs on the pattern of نَامَ يَنَامُ.

109

دَعَا يَدْعُو (To call)

1. The أَلِفٌ with دَعَا is فِعْلٌ مَاضٍ is دَعَا which was originally دَعَوَ. As دَعَا with أَلِفٌ had been softer for the Arabs, they substituted وَاو with أَلِفٌ. The يَدْعُو is فِعْلٌ مُضَارِعٌ, the last letter of which is حَرْفُ الْعِلَّةِ and سَاكِنٌ.

2. The conjugation of 12-D Form دَعَا يَدْعُو is as follows:

اَلنَّهْي	اَلأَمْر	اَلْمُضَارِعُ	اَلْمَاضِي
1. لا تَدْعُ	1. اُدْعُ	1. يَدْعُو	1. دَعَا
2. لا تَدْعُوَا	2. اُدْعُوَا	2. يَدْعُوَان	2. دَعَوَا
3. لا تَدْعُوا	3. اُدْعُوا	3. يَدْعُونَ	3. دَعَوا
4. لا تَدْعِي	4. اُدْعِي	4. تَدْعُو	4. دَعَتْ
5. لا تَدْعُوَا	5. اُدْعُوَا	5. تَدْعُوَان	5. دَعَتَا
6. لا تَدْعُونَ	6. اُدْعُونَ	6. يَدْعُونَ	6. دَعَوْنَ
		7. تَدْعُو	7. دَعَوْتَ
		8. تَدْعُوَان	8. دَعَوْتُمَا
		9. تَدْعُونَ	9. دَعَوْتُمْ
		10. تَدْعِينَ	10. دَعَوْتِ
		11. تَدْعُوَان	11. دَعَوْتُمَا
		12. تَدْعُونَ	12. دَعَوْتُنَّ
		13. أَدْعُو	13 دَعَوْتُ
		14. نَدْعُو	14. دَعَوْنَا

3. **Explanation of the changes in 12-D:** اَلْفِعْلُ الْمَاضِي: دَعَا

   (a) دَعَا is originally دَعَوَ. The Arabs changed دَعَوَ to دَعَا as it was smoother and easier for them to pronounce.

110

(b) On this pattern, the changes from no. 2 to 5 are such that it is better to memorize them the way they are, rather than go deep into the explanation of their intricacies which is something that is not worth the effort. If at no. 2 دَعَوَا, the واو comes from the original form دَعَوَ instead of دَعَا, and in no. 3 دَعَوا it disappears, it is because the Arabs have been pronouncing them like this since time immemorial.

(c) At no. 6 دَعَوْنَ, the original و of دَعَوَ appears and continues till no. 14.

4. **Explanation of the changes in 12-D:** الْفِعْلُ الْمُضَارِعُ: يَدْعُو

No change takes place in the conjugation of فِعْلٌ مُضَارِعٌ and all the letters of no. 1. يَدْعُو are retained till no. 14.

5. **Explanation of the changes in 12-D:** فِعْلُ الأَمْرِ : اُدْعُ

(a) فِعْلُ الأَمْرِ is derived from فِعْلٌ مُضَارِعٌ : يَدْعُو.

(b) The second letter د in يَدْعُو is سَاكِنٌ so أَلِف is introduced for فِعْلُ الأَمْرِ. Its تَشْكِيلٌ is determined by the third letter عُ Since it has *damma*, the أَلِف is given ضَمَّةٌ, hence: اُدْعُو.

(c) The *last* letter of فِعْلُ الأَمْرِ is to be *vowelless*. In اُدْعُو you find the و already having سُكُونٌ.

(d) Giving this و the سُكُونٌ of فِعْلُ الأَمْرِ necessitates the dropping of واو altogether. The omission of this واو amounts to giving it سُكُونٌ. Thus اُدْعُو becomes : اُدْعُ.

(e) In اُدْعُ: فِعْلُ الأَمْرِ you may find ضَمَّةٌ on the last letter but it is considered سَاكِنٌ because "the dropping of واو" gives اُدْعُ the 'vowelless status.'

Thus : اُدْعُ - اُدْعُوَا - اُدْعُوا - اُدْعِي - اُدْعُوَا and اُدْعُونَ.

6. **Explanation of the changes in 12-D:** فِعْلُ النَّهِي : لا تَدْعُ

(a) فِعْلُ النَّهِي depends on فِعْلُ الأَمْرِ for its shape.

111

(b) In اُدْعُ, you prefix 'لاَ' and تَ with *fatha'* making it لاَ تَدْعُ.

(c) The last letter of فِعْلُ النَّهْيِ is سَاكِنْ. In لاَ تَدْعُ the symbol of سُكُونْ is: *"dropping of the weak letter واو"*. Thus لاَ تَدْعُ is *vowelless*.

7. Commonly used verbs on the pattern of 12-D : دَعَا يَدْعُو

    (1)   نَمَا يَنْمُو = to grow

    (2)   عَلاَ يَعْلُو = to rise high

    (3)   سَمَا يَسْمُو = to be high, to tower up

    (4)   رَجَا يَرْجُو = to hope, to expect

    (5)   خَطَا يَخْطُو = to step, to pace

    (6)   دَنَا يَدْنُو = to come or go near

    (7)   بَدَا يَبْدُو = to appear

    (8)   شَكَا يَشْكُو = to complain

    (9)   تَلاَ يَتْلُو = to recite, to read

    (10)   طَهَا يَطْهُو = to cook, to fry

Before moving on to the next Section, make sure you have memorized at least one set of conjugations. Loudly practise the conjugations of the verbs mentioned above. Make ten sentences using these verbs.

$$\boxed{\text{EXERCISE}}$$

FOR SECTION: 12-C نَامَ يَنَامُ AND
SECTION: 12-D دَعَا يَدْعُو

Grammatically analyse the following sentences:

1.   The mother said to the child: "Don't be afraid of the cat."

قَالَتِ الأُمُّ لِلطِّفْلِ: "لاَ تَخَفْ مِنَ الْقِطِّ".

2.   The boy said to his mother: "I have got the first prize".

112

قَالَ الْوَلَدُ لِوَالِدَيْهِ: "قَدْ نِلْتُ الْجَائِزَةَ الْأُولَى".

3. The gardener said to the child: "This plant will grow and become tall after a month."

قَالَ الْبُسْتَانِيُّ لِلطِّفْلِ: "سَتَنْمُو وَ تَعْلُو هَذِهِ الشَّجَرَةُ بَعْدَ شَهْرٍ".

4. I called the servant and said to him: "Wash the cup."

دَعَوْتُ الْخَادِمَ وَقُلْتُ لَهُ: "اِغْسِلْ الْفِنْجَانَ".

5. Does your father recite the Qur'an in the morning?

هَلْ يَتْلُو أَبُوكَ الْقُرْآنَ فِي الصَّبَاحِ؟

GRAMMATICAL ANALYSIS

"الْفِنْجَانَ"	"اِغْسِلْ	لَهُ:	قُلْتُ	وَ	الْخَادِمَ	دَعَوْتُ
↓	↓	↓	↓	↓	↓	↓
الْمَفْعُولُ	اَلْفِعْلُ الصَّحِيحُ	حَرْفُ	اَلْفِعْلُ	حَرْفُ	الْمَفْعُولُ	اَلْفِعْلُ
↓	↓	الْجَرِّ	الْمَاضِي	الْعَطْفِ	↓	الْمَاضِي
اَلتَّشْكِيلُ:	فِعْلُ الْأَمْرِ	↓	↓		اَلتَّشْكِيلُ:	↓
فَتْحَةٌ	↓	مَجْرُورٌ	اَلْفَاعِلُ:		فَتْحَةٌ	اَلْفِعْلُ
↓	اَلْفَاعِلُ:	↓	أَنَا			الْمُعْتَلُّ
الْمَعْرِفَةُ	أَنْتَ	ضَمِيرٌ				↓
		مُتَّصِلٌ				اَلْفَاعِلُ: أَنَا

INSTRUCTIONS

Loudly recite the conjugations of each weak verb found in these sentences.

THE FORM : جَرَى يَجْري (To Run)

1. In the conjugation of the Weak Verb جَرَى يَجْري you will observe that the prefixes and suffixes of مَاضٍ, مُضَارِعٌ, أَمْرٌ and نَهْيٌ, as discussed earlier are the same.

2. Wherever اِجْتِمَاعُ السَّاكِنَيْن happens, changes in the form of omission or التَّشْكِيلُ take place.

3. The conjugations for 12-E Form are:

النَّهْيُ	الأَمْرُ	اَلْمُضَارِعُ	اَلْمَاضِي
1. لاَ تَجْر	1. اِجْرِ	1. يَجْري	1. جَرَى
2. لاَ تَجْرِيَا	2. اِجْرِيَا	2. يَجْرِيَان	2. جَرَيَا
3. لاَ تَجْرُوا	3. اِجْرُوا	3. يَجْرُونَ	3. جَرَوا
4. لاَ تَجْرِي	4. اِجْرِي	4. تَجْري	4. جَرَتْ
5. لاَ تَجْرِيَا	5. اِجْرِيَا	5. تَجْرِيَان	5. جَرَتَا
6. لاَ تَجْرِينَ	6. اِجْرِينَ	6. يَجْرِينَ	6. جَرَيْنَ
		7. تَجْري	7. جَرَيْتَ
		8. تَجْرِيَان	8. جَرَيْتُمَا
		9. تَجْرُونَ	9. جَرَيْتُمْ
		10. تَجْرِينَ	10. جَرَيْتِ
		11. تَجْرِيَان	11. جَرَيْتُمَا
		12. تَجْرِينَ	12. جَرَيْتُنَّ
		13. أَجْري	13. جَرَيْتُ
		14. نَجْري	14. جَرَيْنَا

4. **Explanation of the 12-E changes in اَلْفِعْلُ اَلْمَاضِى: جَرَى.**

114

In the conjugation of مَاضٍ you observe that as in the case دَعَا, the form stabilizes at no: 6 جَرَيْنَ and moves on retaining the original ي on this pattern as it is *not* causing اِجْتِمَاعُ السَّاكِنَيْنِ.

5. **Explanation of the 12-E changes in اَلْفِعْلُ الْمُضَارِعُ**: يَجْرِي.

No omission of the حَرْفُ الْعِلَّةِ: ي takes place, as there is no اِجْتِمَاعُ السَّاكِنَيْنِ.

6. **Explanation of the 12-E changes in فِعْلُ الأَمْرِ**: اِجْرِ.

(a) فِعْلُ الأَمْرِ depends on اَلْفِعْلُ الْمُضَارِعُ for its form.

(b) As the *second* letter of يَجْرِي is سَاكِنٌ, the أَلِفٌ is introduced as prefix for فِعْلُ الأَمْرِ as: اِجرِىْ.

(c) The *third* letter of يَجْرِي determines the vowel mark of the prefix أَلِفٌ. As it is *kasra*, it is given to this أَلِفٌ making it اِجرِي.

(d) The dropping of the final حَرْفُ الْعِلَّةِ: ي amounts to giving سُكُونٌ to such فِعْلُ الأَمْرِ. Thus: اِجْرِ.

7. **Explanation of the 12-E changes in فِعْلُ النَّهْيِ**: لاَتَجْرِ.

As فِعْلُ النَّهْيِ is dependent for its shape on the فِعْلُ الأَمْرِ and only ' لاَ ' and تَ with *fatha*' is prefixed instead of أَلِفٌ, whatever change happens in الأَمْرِ, it occurs in فِعْلُ النَّهْيِ too.

Thus: لاَ تَجْرِ-لاَ تَجْرِيَا-لاَ تَجْرُوا-لاَ تَجْرِي-لاَ تَجْرِيَا and لاَ تَجْرِينَ.

8. Commonly used weak verbs similar to جَرَى يَجْرِي of SECTION : 12-E are :

النَّهْيُ	الأَمْرُ	اَلْمُضَارِعُ	اَلْمَاضِي		
لا تَبْكِ	اِبْكِ	يَبْكِي	بَكَى	:	to weep.	(1)
لا تَأْتِ	اِئْتِ	يَأْتِي	أَتَى	:	to come.	(2)
لا تَمْشِ	اِمْشِ	يَمْشِي	مَشَى	:	to walk.	(3)
لا تَطْوِ	اِطْوِ	يَطْوِي	طَوَى	:	to fold.	(4)

115

(5)	لا تَبْنِ اِبْنِ	يَبْنِي	بَنَى	: to build.
(6)	لا تَسْقِ اِسْقِ	يَسْقِي	سَقَى	: to irrigate.
(7)	لا تَجْنِ اِجْنِ	يَجْنِي	جَنَى	: to pick, gather.
(8)	لا تَبْرِ اِبْرِ	يَبْرِي	بَرَى	: to sharpen.
(9)	لا تَرْمِ اِرْمِ	يَرْمِي	رَمَى	: to throw.
(10)	لا تَمْضِ اِمْضِ	يَمْضِي	مَضَى	: to pass.

INSTRUCTIONS

Memorize the above mentioned verbs on the pattern of the جَرَى يَجْرِي.

لَقِيَ يَلْقَى (TO MEET)

1. In this section of the weak verb لَقِيَ يَلْقَى too, you shall find that all the prefixes and suffixes of مَاضٍ, مُضَارِعٌ, أَمْرٌ and نَهْيٌ are similar to those discussed earlier.

2. Wherever اِجْتِمَاعُ السَّاكِنَيْنِ takes place, changes in the form of omission or تَشْكِيلٌ occur.

3. The conjugations for the 12-F Form are:

اَلنَّهْيُ	اَلْأَمْرُ	اَلْمُضَارِعُ	اَلْمَاضِي
1. لا تَلْقَ	1. اِلْقَ	1. يَلْقَى	1. لَقِيَ
2. لا تَلْقَيَا	2. اِلْقَيَا	2. يَلْقَيَان	2. لَقِيَا
3. لا تَلْقَوْا	3. اِلْقَوْا	3. يَلْقَوْنَ	3. لَقُوا
4. لا تَلْقَيْ	4. اِلْقَيْ	4. تَلْقَى	4. لَقِيَتْ
5. لا تَلْقَيَا	5. اِلْقَيَا	5. تَلْقَيَان	5. لَقِيَتَا
6. لا تَلْقَيْنَ	6. اِلْقَيْنَ	6. يَلْقَيْنَ	6. لَقِينَ
		7. تَلْقَى	7. لَقِيتَ
		8. تَلْقَيَان	8. لَقِيتُمَا
		9. تَلْقَوْنَ	9. لَقِيتُمْ
		10. تَلْقَيْنَ	10. لَقِيتِ
		11. تَلْقَيَان	11. لَقِيتُمَا
		12. تَلْقَيْنَ	12. لَقِيتُنَّ
		13. أَلْقَى	13. لَقِيتُ
		14. نَلْقَى	14. لَقِينَا

4. **Explanation of the 12-F changes in المَاضِي and المُضَارِعُ:**

117

لَقِــيَ يَلْقَــى: These two conjugations move or retaining the حَرْفُ الْعِلَّـةِ at most places. Wherever they do not, they should be memorized as such because the description of such rare changes is found to be less than fully convincing to the students and therefore it should better be avoided at this stage.

5. **Explanation of the 12-F changes in فِعْلُ الْأَمْرِ and فِعْلُ النَّهْيِ: اِلْقَ - لا تَلْقَ**

(a) فِعْلُ الْأَمْرِ: اِلْقَ owes its shape to يَلْقَى. The *second* letter of يَلْقَى is vowelless, so أَلِـف as a *prefix* is introduced. Its تَشْكِيلٌ is determined by the third letter of يَلْقَى. Its تَشْكِيلٌ has *fatha*. This *fatha* cannot be given to أَلِف, because in three-letter verbs it is *not allowed*. Instead *kasra* is given making it: اِلْقَــى. The *omission of* the weak letter ي amounts to giving سُكُونٌ to فِعْلُ الْأَمْرِ.

Thus : اِلْقَ - اِلْقَيَا - اِلْقَوْا - اِلْقَي - اِلْقَيَا - اِلْقَيْنَ.

(b) In فِعْلُ النَّهْيِ, the prefix of اِلْقَ is substituted with 'لاَ' and ت with *fatha*'.

Thus: لا تَلْقَ, لا تَلْقَيَا, لا تَلْقَوْا, لا تَلْقَى, لا تَلْقَيَا and لا تَلْقَيْنَ.

6. Commonly used verbs identified on the pattern of لَقِيَ يَلْقَى are:

اَلْمَاضِي	اَلْمُضَارِعُ		
1.	خَشِيَ	يَخْشَى	= to fear, to dread.
2.	بَقِيَ	يَبْقَى	= to remain, continue to be.
3.	خَفِيَ	يَخْفَى	= to be hidden or concealed.
4.	غَنِيَ	يَغْنَى	= to be rich.
5.	رَضِيَ	يَرْضَى	= to be pleased or content.
6.	رَوِيَ	يَرْوَى	= to quench one's thirst.
7.	قَوِيَ	يَقْوَى	= to be or become strong.

118

8. أَذِيَ يَأْذَى = to be harmed.

— Memorize the conjugations of the above mentioned verbs on the pattern of لَقِيَ يَلْقَى.

— Check whether the conjugations beginning from Section 12-A are memorized. Read these *six* sections several times and repeat the conjugations till you perfect them.

$$\boxed{\text{EXERCISE}}$$

FOR SECTION 12-E لَقِيَ يَلْقَى AND SECTION 12-F جَرَى يَجْرِي

Grammatically analyse the following sentences:

1. The child fell on the ground so he wept.

سَقَطَ الطِّفْلُ عَلَى الأَرْضِ فَبَكَى.

2. After the dinner I walk in the garden with my son.

بَعْدَ الْعَشَاءِ أَمْشِي فِي الْحَدِيقَةِ مَعَ اِبْنِي.

3. The teacher said to the student: "Sharpen the pencil."

قَالَ الْمُدَرِّسُ لِلتِّلْمِيذِ : اِبْرِ قَلَمَ الرَّصَاصِ.

4. I did not meet Majid in his office today.

مَا لَقِيتُ مَاجِداً فِي مَكْتَبِهِ الْيَوْمَ.

5. I remained in my house due to rain. بَقِيتُ فِي بَيْتِي بِسَبَبِ الْمَطَرِ.

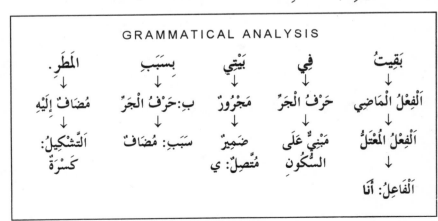

119

1. بَقِيتُ = is اَلْفِعْلُ الْمَاضِي on the pattern of 12-F and 'the doer' is أَنَا.

2. فِي = is a preposition . It is مَبْنِيٌّ, that is *indeclinable*.

3. بَيْتِي = is a 'noun governed by a preposition' or مَجْرُورٌ, and ي is 'personal pronoun possessive' or ضَمِيرٌ مُتَّصِلٌ.

4. بِسَبَبِ = ب is a preposition, and سَبَبِ is مَجْرُورٌ and مُضَافٌ.

5. الْمَطَرِ = is مُضَافٌ إِلَيْهِ and therefore its vowel mark is كَسْرَةٌ

INSTRUCTIONS

Check whether the conjugations beginning from Section-A are memorized. Read these *six* sections several times and repeat the conjugations till you perfect them.

وَجَدَ يَجِدُ (TO FIND)

1. In the conjugation of the weak verb وَجَدَ يَجِدُ, you will observe that the prefixes and suffixes of اَلْمَاضِي, اَلْمُضَارِعُ, الأَمْرُ and النَّهْيُ *do not undergo* any change .

2. The conjugations for 12-G Form run as follows:

النَّهْيُ	اَلأَمْرُ	اَلْمُضَارِعُ	اَلْمَاضِي
1. لا تَجِدْ	1. جِدْ	1. يَجِدُ	1. وَجَدَ
2. لا تَجِدَا	2. جِدَا	2. يَجِدَانِ	2. وَجَدَا
3. لا تَجِدُوا	3. جِدُوا	3. يَجِدُونَ	3. وَجَدُوا
4. لا تَجِدِي	4. جِدِي	4. تَجِدُ	4. وَجَدَتْ
5. لا تَجِدَا	5. جِدَا	5. تَجِدَانِ	5. وَجَدَتَا
6. لا تَجِدْنَ	6. جِدْنَ	6. يَجِدْنَ	6. وَجَدْنَ
		7. تَجِدُ	7. وَجَدْتَ
		8. تَجِدَانِ	8. وَجَدْتُمَا
		9. تَجِدُونَ	9. وَجَدْتُمْ
		10. تَجِدِينَ	10. وَجَدْتِ
		11. تَجِدَانِ	11. وَجَدْتُمَا
		12. تَجِدْنَ	12. وَجَدْتُنَّ
		13. أَجِدُ	13. وَجَدْتُ
		14. نَجِدُ	14. وَجَدْنَا

3. **Explanation of the 12-G conjugation in اَلْفِعْل اَلْمَاضِي: وَجَدَ**
   In this conjugation, no اِجْتِمَاعُ السَّاكِنَيْنِ occurs and thus there is *no change* anywhere.

4. **Explanation of the 12-G conjugation in اَلْفِعْل الْمُضَارِعُ : يَجِدُ**
   (a) If a triliteral verb in اَلْمَاضِي has و as its *first* letter and فَتْحَةٌ

121

on *all its three* letters, it is *dropped* in الْمُضَارِعُ. Thus it becomes يَجِدُ and *not* يَوْجِدُ.

(b) *No change* occurs in the conjugation of يَجِدُ as there is no اِجْتِمَاعُ السَّاكِنَيْنِ (the coming together of two vowelless letters).

5. **Explanation of the 12-G conjugation in** جِدْ : فِعْلُ الأَمْرِ

(a) فِعْلُ الأَمْرِ is derived from اَلْفِعْلُ الْمُضَارِعُ for its form.

(b) If the *second letter* of يَجِدُ is *not* سَاكِنْ *vowelless*, as is the case here, *no* أَلِف is introduced as prefix for فِعْلُ الأَمْرِ.

(c) Instead يَ, the *prefix* of الْمُضَارِعُ is *dropped*.

(d) It becomes جِدُ.

(e) The *last* letter is given سُكُونْ making it جِدْ.

(f) And the conjugation runs as: جِدْ, جِدَا, جِدُوا, جِدِي, جِدَا, and جِدْنَ. No changes take place here.

6. **Explanation of the 12-G conjugation in** لاَ تَجِدْ : فِعْلُ النَّهْيِ

(a) As فِعْلُ النَّهْيِ depends on فِعْلُ الأَمْرِ for its form, لاَ and تَ are prefixed to فِعْلُ الأَمْرِ and the conjugation runs as: لاَ تَجِدْ, لاَ تَجِدَا, لاَ تَجِدُوا, لاَ تَجِدِي, لاَ تَجِدَا, and لاَ تَجِدْنَ. No changes take place here.

7. Commonly used verbs on the pattern of 12-G:

(1) وَضَعَ - يَضَعُ = to put, to place.

(2) وَقَعَ - يَقَعُ = to be situated, to fall.

(3) وَرَدَ - يَرِدُ = to come, to arrive.

(4) وَزَنَ - يَزِنُ = to weigh.

(5) وَصَفَ - يَصِفُ = to describe.

(6) وَعَدَ - يَعِدُ = to promise.

(7) وَقَفَ - يَقِفُ = to stop, to stand.

(8) وَصَلَ - يَصِلُ = to arrive, to reach.

وَقَى يَقِي (TO PROTECT, TO GUARD)

1. In the conjugation of the Weak verb وَقَى يَقِي , you shall observe that the prefixes and suffixes of اَلْمَاضِي, اَلْمُضَارِعُ, اَلْأَمْرُ and اَلنَّهْيُ *do not* undergo any change.

2. The Conjugation for the 12-H Form are as follows :

اَلنَّهْيُ	اَلْأَمْرُ	اَلْمُضَارِعُ	اَلْمَاضِي
1. لا تَقِ	1. قِ	1. يَقِي	1. وَقَى
2. لا تَقِيَا	2. قِيَا	2. يَقِيَان	2. وَقَيَا
3. لا تَقُوا	3. قُوا	3. يَقُونَ	3. وَقَوا
4. لا تَقِي	4. قِي	4. تَقِي	4. وَقَتْ
5. لا تَقِيَا	5. قِيَا	5. تَقِيَان	5. وَقَتَا
6. لا تَقِينَ	6. قِينَ	6. يَقِينَ	6. وَقَيْنَ
		7. تَقِي	7. وَقَيْتَ
		8. تَقِيَان	8. وَقَيْتُما
		9. تَقُونَ	9. وَقَيْتُمْ
		10. تَقِينَ	10. وَقَيْتِ
		11. تَقِيان	11. وَقَيْتُمَا
		12. تَقِينَ	12. وَقَيْتُنَّ
		13. أَقِي	13. وَقَيْتُ
		14. نَقِي	14. وَقَيْنَا

3. **Explanation of the 12-H conjugation in** اَلْمَاضِي **and** اَلْمُضَارِعُ: وَقَى يَقِي

These two conjugations move on retaining the weak letter ي at most places. Wherever they do not, they should be memorized as such because the explanation of such changes is found to be

123

less than fully convincing to the student and therefore it should be avoided at this stage.

4. **Explanation of 12-H conjugation in ٱلأَمْرُ: قِ**

   (a) فِعْلُ الأَمْرِ depends on ٱلْفِعْلُ الْمُضَارِعُ for its form.

   (b) As you can see the second letter of ٱلْفِعْلُ الْمُضَارِعُ : يَقِيْ is not vowelless, therefore no أَلِفٌ is introduced as prefix for فِعْلُ الأَمْرِ.

   (c) Instead ي, the prefix of ٱلْمُضَارِعُ is dropped.

   (d) It becomes قِيْ.

   (e) The last letter of فِعْلُ الأَمْرِ must be vowelless.
   In قِيْ , you find the ي already having سُكُونْ.

   (f) Giving this ي the سُكُونْ of فِعْلُ الأَمْرِ necessitates *dropping* of the ي altogether. The omission of this ي *amounts to* giving سُكُونْ. Thus قِيْ becomes قِ (protect!).

   (g) In قِ :فِعْلُ الأَمْرِ you find كَسْرَةٌ on the only remaining letter قِ, but it is regarded سَاكِنٌ because the dropping of the weak letter ي gives قِ the "vowelless status".
   Thus: قِ - قِيَا - قُوا - قِي - قِيَ and قِينَ.

5. **Explanation of 12-H conjugation in النَّهِي: لا تَقِ**

   As فِعْلُ النَّهِي depends on فِعْلُ الأَمْرِ for its form, لاَ and تَ are prefixed to فِعْلُ الأَمْرِ and the conjugation runs as: لا تَقِ, لا تَقِيَا, لا تَقُوا, لا تَقِي, لا تَقِيَا and لا تَقِينَ.

6. Commonly used verbs on the pattern of 12-H : وَقَى يَقِي

   (1) وَفَى يَفِي (بـ) = to live up (to a promise), to fulfill.

   (2) وَشَى يَشِي = to embellish, to defame.

   (3) وَعَى يَعِي = to remember, to know by heart, to know.

   (4) وَنَى يَنِي = to become weak or tired.

124

FOR SECTION 12-H وَجَدَ يَجِدُ AND SECTION 12-G وَقَى يَقِي

Grammatically analyse the following sentences:

1. Where is your office situated?　أَيْنَ يَقَعُ مَكْتَبُكَ ؟

2. My office is situated in the old city.　يَقَعُ مَكْتَبِي فِي الْمَدِينَةِ الْقَدِيمَةِ.

3. Please put the letter in an envelope.

مِنْ فَضْلِكَ ، ضَعِ الْخِطَابَ فِي ظَرْفٍ.

4. The bag protected the book and the notebook from the rain.

وَقَتِ الْحَقِيبَةُ الْكِتَابَ وَالْكُرَّاسَةَ مِنَ الْمَطَرِ.

5. I have fulfilled my promise .　قَدْ وَفَيْتُ بِوَعْدِي.

GRAMMATICAL ANALYSIS

مِنْ	فَضْلِكَ،	ضَعِ	الْخِطَابَ	فِي	ظَرْفٍ.
1.	2.	3.	4.	5.	6.
حَرْفُ جَرٍّ	مَجْرُورٌ	فِعْلٌ مُعْتَلٌّ	مَفْعُولٌ	حَرْفُ جَرٍّ	مَجْرُورٌ
↓	↓	↓	↓	↓	↓
مَبْنِيٌّ عَلَى	كَ: ضَمِيرٌ	فِعْلُ الْأَمْرِ	اَلتَّشْكِيلُ:		اَلتَّشْكِيلُ:
السُّكُون	مُتَّصِلٌ	↓	فَتْحَةً		كَسْرَةٌ
		وَالْفَاعِلُ: أَنتَ			

125

The Weak Verb In A Nutshell

Eight kinds of weak verbs were discussed in this lesson:

(1) Those on the pattern of قَالَ, يَقُولُ, قُلْ and لَا تَقُلْ like: قَامَ, زَارَ, and عَادَ etc. صَامَ, سَاقَ, سَادَ, دَارَ, فَازَ, طَافَ, تَابَ

(2) Those on the pattern of بَاعَ, يَبِيعُ, بِعْ, and لا تَبِعْ like: غَابَ, مَالَ, and عَاشَ etc. صَادَ, جَاءَ, سَارَ, طَارَ, سَالَ, صَاحَ, طَابَ

(3) Those on the pattern of نَامَ, يَنَامُ, نَمْ, and لا تَنَمْ like: خَافَ, نَالَ, and هَابَ etc.

(4) Weak verbs on the pattern of دَعَا, يَدْعُو اُدْعُ and لا تَدْعُ like: and طَهَا etc. نَمَا, عَلاَ, سَمَا, رَجَا, خَطَا, دَنَا, بَدَا, شَكَا, تَلاَ

(5) The fifth category of weak verbs comes on the pattern of جَرَى, رَمَى, بَكَى, أَتَى, مَشَى, طَوَى, بَنَى, سَقَى, يَجْرِي اِجْرِ and لا تَجْرِ like: and مَضَى etc. جَنَى, بَرَى, رَمَى

(6) The verbs on the pattern of لَقِيَ, يَلْقَي اِلْقَ and لا تَلْقَ like: خَشِيَ, and أَذِيَ etc. بَقِيَ, خَفِيَ, رَوِيَ, قَوِيَ, غَنِيَ, رَضِيَ

(7) The verbs on the pattern of وَجَدَ, يَجِدُ, جِدْ, and لا تَجِدْ like: and وَصَلَ etc. وَضَعَ, وَقَعَ, وَرَدَ, وَزَنَ, وَصَفَ, وَعَدَ, وَقَفَ

(8) The verbs on the pattern of وَقَى, يَقِي, قِ, and لاتَقِ like: وَفَى, and وَنَى etc. وَشَى, وَعَى

126

ظَرْفُ الزَّمان
The Adverb Of Time
❦

EXAMPLE

I will come tomorrow.   سَأَجِئُ   غَدًا.
↓   ↓
ADVERB OF TIME   ZARFUZ-ZAMAANI
↓
ظَرْفُ الزَّمَان

---

1. Those words through which *'time'* or *'period'* is expressed like 'today' and 'tomorrow' are called the ظُرُوفُ الزَّمَانِ *zuruufuz-zamaani*.

2. In Arabic, *"in the morning"* can be said in *two* ways: فِي الصَّبَاح as preposition and the noun governed by the preposition, *or* as صَبَاحًا with *fatha*.

3. This word صَبَاحًا is then called ظَرْفُ الزّمانِ *zarfuz-zamaani* (the adverb of time).

4. There is *no* difference in the meaning of فِي الصَّبَاح and صَبَاحًا.

5. Barring a few, most of these ظُرُوفُ الزَّمَان carry *fatha*.

6. The commonly used ظُرُوفُ الزّمان are:

   (1) اَلْيَوْمَ : today.

   (2) غدًا : tomorrow.

   (3) أَمْسِ : yesterday (with fixed *kasra*).

   (4) ظُهْرًا : at noon.

   (5) مَسَاءً : in the evening.

127

(6)	لَيْلاً	:	at night.
(7)	نَهَاراً	:	during/in the day.
(8)	أَحْيَاناً	:	sometimes.

7. The following are used as مُضَافٌ and therefore the noun *following* them gets *kasra*:

(1)	قَبْلَ	:	before.
(2)	بَعْدَ	:	after.
(3)	خِلالَ	:	during.
(4)	كُلَّ يَوْمٍ	:	every day.
(5)	كُلَّ أُسْبُوعٍ	:	every week.
(6)	كُلَّ شَهْرٍ	:	every month.
(7)	كُلَّ عَامٍ	:	every year.
(8)	ذاتَ يَوْمٍ	:	one day.

8. The following combinations appear as صِفَةٌ and مَوْصُوفٌ :

(1)	اَلأُسْبُوعَ الْقَادِمَ	=	next week
(2)	اَلأُسْبُوعَ الْمَاضِيَ	=	last week
(3)	الشَّهْرَ الْقَادِمَ	=	next month
(4)	اَلْعَامَ الْقَادِمَ	=	next year

EXERCISE

Grammatically analyse the following sentences:

1. I will visit him in Cairo *next year*.

سَوْفَ أَزُورُهُ فِي الْقَاهِرَةِ اَلْعَامَ الْقَادِمَ.

2. She will return from her office *in the evening*.

سَتَرْجِعُ مِنْ مَكْتَبِهَا مَسَاءً.

3. His brother will return from America *next week*.

سَيَعُودُ أَخُوهُ مِنْ أَمْرِيكَا اَلأُسْبُوعَ الْقَادِمَ.

128

4. Do you read the Arabic newspaper *in the morning*?

هَلْ تَقْرَأُ الْجَرِيدَةَ الْعَرَبِيَّةَ صَبَاحاً؟

5. No, I read the English newspaper *in the morning*.

لا، أَنَا أَقْرَأُ الْجَرِيدَةَ الإِنْكِلِيزِيَّةَ صَبَاحاً.

GRAMMATICAL ANALYSIS

سَوْفَ	أَزُورُهُ	فِي	الْقَاهِرَةِ	اَلْعَامَ الْقَادِمَ.
↓	↓	↓	↓	↓
حَرْفٌ	اَلْفِعْلُ الْمُضَارِعُ	حَرْفُ	مَجْرُورٌ	ظَرْفُ الزَّمَان
الإِسْتِقْبَال	↓	الْجَرِّ		↓
↓	اَلْفِعْلُ الْمُعْتَلُّ			مَوْصُوفٌ
مَبْنِيٌّ عَلَى	↓			↓
الْفَتْحَةِ	اَلْفَاعِلُ: أَنَا			صِفَةٌ
	↓			↓
	الْمَفْعُولُ: ه			اَلتَّشْكِيلُ:
	ضَمِيرٌ مُتَّصِلٌ			فَتْحَةٌ

---

(1) سَوْفَ: is called the حَرْفُ الإِسْتِقْبَال (*harfu'l-istiqbaali*) and it precedes اَلْفِعْلُ الْمُضَارِعُ to turn it into a *future* tense verb.

(2) أَزُورُهُ: is اَلْفِعْلُ الْمُعْتَلُّ or the 'weak verb' as it contains واو, the حَرْفُ الْعِلَّةِ. The 'doer' is the in-built أَنَا. And الْمَفْعُولُ is ه the ضَمِيرٌ مُتَّصِلٌ (I will visit *him*).

(3) فِي: is حَرْفُ الْجَرِّ which gives *kasra* to the noun coming *after* it. And فِي is مَبْنِيٌّ that is: it has a *fixed* تَشْكِيلٌ: سُكُونْ.

(4) الْقَاهِرَةِ: is مَجْرُورٌ, the تَشْكِيلٌ of which is *kasra*.

(5) اَلْعَامَ الْقَادِمَ: ظَرْفُ الزَّمَان expresses 'time' therefore it is regarded and carries *fatha*. It is also صِفَةٌ and مَوْصُوفٌ.

ظَرْفُ الْمَكَان

The Adverb Of Place

❧❦❧

	EXAMPLE	
The book is over the table.		اَلْكِتَابُ فَوْقَ الطَّاوِلَةِ .
↓		↓
ADVERB OF PLACE		ZARFUL-MAKAANI
		↓
		ظَرْفُ المَكَان

---

1. In Arabic, the words like *behind, under* and *over* etc. are called ظُرُوفُ المَكَان (*zuruuful-makaani*), the '*adverbs of place*'. (The singular is: ظَرْفُ المَكَان *zarful-makaani*).

2. Except when preceded by a *preposition*, most 'adverbs of place' carry *fatha*. For example: فَوْقَ meaning: *over*.

3. Most ظُرُوفُ المَكَان are shaped as مُضَافٌ and therefore the noun *following* them is مُضَافٌ إلَيْهِ, which carries '*kasra*'.

4. Thus: "The book is *over* the table" is: اَلْكِتَابُ فَوْقَ الطَّاوِلَةِ .

5. In this sentence, اَلْكِتَابُ is the 'subject' and فَوْقَ الطَّاوِلَةِ is the 'predicate' which consists of ظَرْفُ المَكَان: فَوْقَ as مُضَافٌ and الطَّاوِلَةِ as مُضَافٌ إلَيْهِ, the 'case ending' of which is *kasra*.

6. Some commonly used *adverbs of place* used as مُضَافٌ are:

    (1) تَحْتَ = under   (5) قُرْبَ = near

    (2) خَلْفَ = at the back of   (6) فَوْقَ = over

    (3) وَرَاءَ = behind   (7) بَيْنَ = between

    (4) أَمَامَ = in front of   (8) بِجِوَارِ = beside

7. The following adverbs are 'indeclinable':

(1) هُنَا = here

(2) هُنَاكَ = there

EXERCISE

Grammatically analyse these sentences:

1. She said to me:"The manager lives *behind* that yellow house."

قَالَتْ لِي :"يَسْكُنُ الْمُدِيرُ وَرَاءَ ذَلِكَ الْبَيْتِ الأَصْفَرِ" .

2. *In front of* the university (there) is a bus-stand.

أَمَامَ الْجَامِعَةِ مَوْقِفُ بَاصٍ.

3. The engineer left his bag *under* the table.

تَرَكَ الْمُهَنْدِسُ حَقِيبَتَهُ تَحْتَ الطَّاوِلَةِ.

4. *At the back of* the college there is a big field.

خَلْفَ الْكُلِّيَّةِ مَيْدَانٌ كَبِيرٌ.

5. There is a small window *by the side of* the door.

بِجِوَارِ الْبَابِ نَافِذَةٌ صَغِيرَةٌ.

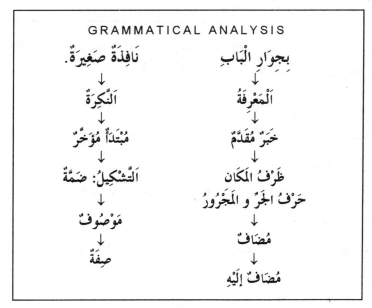

131

1. بِجِوَارِ الْبَابِ = خَبَرٌ مُقَدَّمٌ is because : "There is a small window" is *an indefinite subject* and therefore the sentence in Arabic cannot begin with نَافِذَةٌ صَغِيرَةٌ. This خَبَرٌ مُقَدَّمٌ has two parts (1) ظَرْفُ الْمَكَانِ which has a preposition بِ and called بِجِوَار and (2) مُضَافٌ is الْبَابِ and مُضَافٌ and مَجْرُورٌ as جِوَار.

2. نَافِذَةٌ صَغِيرَةٌ = مُبْتَدَأٌ مُؤَخَّرٌ is or the *'delayed subject'* which must appear *after* the خَبَرٌ مُقَدَّمٌ because it is نَكِرَةٌ or *indefinite*. Here it comprises of صِفَةٌ and مَوْصُوفٌ.

MORE ANALYSIS

تَرَكَ	الْمُهَنْدِسُ	حَقِيبَتَهُ	تَحْتَ	الطَّاوِلَةِ.
↓	↓	↓	↓	↓
اَلْفِعْلُ الصَّحِيحُ	اَلْفَاعِلُ	اَلْمَفْعُولُ	ظَرْفُ الْمَكَانِ	مُضَافٌ إِلَيْهِ
↓	↓	↓	↓	↓
اَلْفِعْلُ الْمَاضِي	اَلتَّشْكِيلُ: ضَمَّةٌ	اَلتَّشْكِيلُ: فَتْحَةٌ	اَلتَّشْكِيلُ: فَتْحَةٌ	اَلتَّشْكِيلُ: كَسْرَةٌ
		↓	↓	
		ضَمِيرٌ مُتَّصِلٌ: هُ	مُضَافٌ	

---

1. تَرَكَ = is a 'strong verb' or الفِعْلُ الصَّحِيحُ (*al-fi 'lus-sahiihu*) and it is اَلْفِعْلُ الْمَاضِي.

2. الْمُهَنْدِسُ = is اَلْفَاعِلُ, the vowel mark of which is ضَمَّةٌ.

3. حَقِيبَتَهُ = is الْمَفْعُولُ, the تَشْكِيلٌ of which is فَتْحَةٌ and it has ضَمِيرٌ مُتَّصِلٌ as a suffix.

4. تَحْتَ = is ظَرْفُ الْمَكَانِ, the تَشْكِيلٌ of which is *fatha* and it is مُضَافٌ.

5. الطَّاوِلَةِ = is مُضَافٌ إِلَيْهِ , the تَشْكِيلٌ of which is *kasra*.

132

LESSON FIFTEEN

اَلْفِعْلُ الْمُضَاعَفُ

The Doubled Verb


```
EXAMPLE
مَرَّ (marra)      يَـمُرُّ (yamurru)   =  to pass
      ↓                    ↓
DOUBLED VERB         DOUBLED VERB
```

1. In the above example you find a verb مَرَّ which has a *'doubling sign'* called شَدَّةٌ (*shaddatun*) over رّ.

2. The *doubled verb* like مَرَّ is called اَلْفِعْلُ الْمُضَاعَفُ.

3. اَلْفِعْلُ الْمُضَاعَفُ is that verb in which the second and third letters are *similar* like : مَرَّ .

4. If *two similar* letters with the *same* تَشْكِيلٌ appear immediately after one another, they are *not* written separately like مَرَرَ instead 'the doubling symbol' or شَدَّةٌ is used as in: مَرَّ; and يَمْرُرُ is يَمُرُّ.

5. Some changes occur in the conjugations of such verbs which are being explained after point no. 6.

6. The conjugations of مَرَّ يَمُرُّ : اَلْفِعْلُ الْمُضَاعَفُ (to pass) are:

اَلنَّهْيُ	اَلأَمْرُ	اَلْمُضَارِعُ	اَلْمَاضِي
1. لَا تَمُرَّ	1. مُرَّ	1. يَمُرُّ	1. مَرَّ
2. لَا تَمُرَّا	2. مُرَّا	2. يَمُرَّانِ	2. مَرَّا
3. لَا تَمُرُّوا	3. مُرُّوا	3. يَمُرُّونَ	3. مَرُّوا
4. لَا تَمُرِّي	4. مُرِّي	4. تَمُرُّ	4. مَرَّتْ
5. لَا تَمُرَّا	5. مُرَّا	5. تَمُرَّانِ	5. مَرَّتَا
6. لَا تَمْرُرْنَ	6. أُمْرُرْنَ	6. يَمْرُرْنَ	6. مَرَرْنَ
		7. تَمُرُّ	7. مَرَرْتَ
		8. تَمُرَّانِ	8. مَرَرْتُمَا
		9. تَمُرُّونَ	9. مَرَرْتُمْ
		10. تَمُرِّينَ	10. مَرَرْتِ
		11. تَمُرَّانِ	11. مَرَرْتُمَا
		12. تَمْرُرْنَ	12. مَرَرْتُنَّ
		13. أَمُرُّ	13. مَرَرْتُ
		14. نَمُرُّ	14. مَرَرْنَا

7. **Explanation of the changes of** اَلْفِعْلُ الْمَاضِي : مَرَّ

(a) Such a triliteral doubled verb moves on *unchanged,* that is with شَدَّةٌ, *the doubling sign* upto no. 5.

(b) At number 6, the twin letters ر are *detached* as in مَرَرْنَ.

(c) And they *remain detached* from each other till no. 14.

8. **Explanation of the changes in** اَلْفِعْلُ الْمُضَارِعُ : يَمُرُّ

(a) Except no. 6 and no. 12, the *present tense* doubled verb moves on as originally formed, that is, with شَدَّةٌ

(b) At no. 6 and no. 12, the twin letters ر are *separated* making it يَمْرُرْنَ (instead of يَمُرَّنَ) and تَمْرُرْنَ (instead of تَمُرَّنَ).

134

9. **Explanation of the changes in مُرَّ : فِعْلُ الأَمْرِ**

   (a) Since the *second* letter of the *present tense:* يَمُرُّ is *not* vowelless, no أَلِفٌ is prefixed in فِعْلُ الأَمْرِ, making it: مُرُّ.

   (b) The *last letter* of فِعْلُ الأَمْرِ is to be *vowelless*. The method for making the doubled verb سَاكِنٌ is to give it *fatha*.

   (c) The *fatha* on the last letter of أَلْفِعْلُ الْمُضَاعَفُ is equal to سُكُونٌ. Thus مُرَّ, inspite of *fatha*, is regarded *vowelless*.

   (d) This shape goes on till no. 5 as: مُرِّي - مُرُّوا - مُرَّا - مُرَّ and مُرَّا.

   (e) At no. 6, the فِعْلُ الأَمْرِ is *not* مُرَّنَ, instead it is shaped as though the present tense verb was يَمْرُرُ. Since the second letter here is *vowelless*, the prefix أَلِفٌ is introduced and given *damma* because the third letter has ضَمّةٌ. And the last letter is given سُكُونٌ making it اُمْرُرْ. Thus no. 6 becomes: اُمْرُرْنَ.

10. **Explanation of the changes in فِعْلُ النَّهْي: لا تَمُرَّ.**

    The same six moods of فِعْلُ الأَمْرِ are prefixed with لاَ and تَ with *fatha* in فِعْلُ النَّهْي.

11. Some commonly used 'doubled verbs' are:

    دَقَّ يَدُقُّ (to knock at). شَنَّ يَشُنُّ (to launch).

    فَرَّ يَفِرُّ (to run away). شَمَّ يَشُمُّ (to smell).

    مَرَّ يَمُرُّ (to pass by).

EXERCISE

Grammatically analyse the following sentences:

(1) The bus passed by the main market.

مَرَّتِ الْحَافِلَةُ بِالسُّوقِ الرَّئِيسِيِّ.

(2) Do not smell the yellow flower.　لَا تَشُمَّ الزَّهْرَةَ الصَّفْرَاءَ.

(3) I knocked at the door so the maid servant opened it.

دَقَقْتُ الْبَابَ فَفَتَحَتْهُ الْخَادِمَةُ.

(4) Please knock at the door before you enter.

مِنْ فَضْلِكَ، دُقَّ الْبَابَ قَبْلَ دُخُولِكَ.

(5) The thief escaped in the darkness.　فَرَّ السَّارِقُ فِي الظَّلَامِ.

GRAMMATICAL ANALYSIS

دَقَقْتُ	الْبَابَ	فَفَتَحَتْهُ	الْخَادِمَةُ.
1	2	3	4
↓	↓	↓	↓
اَلْفِعْلُ الْمُضَاعَفُ	اَلْمَفْعُولُ	فَ: حَرْفُ الْعَطْفِ	اَلْفَاعِلُ
↓	↓	↓	↓
اَلْفِعْلُ الْمَاضِي	اَلتَّشْكِيلُ: فَتْحَة	اَلْفِعْلُ الْمَاضِي	اَلتَّشْكِيلُ: ضَمَّة
↓		↓	
اَلْفَاعِلُ: أَنَا		الْمَفْعُولُ: هُ	
		↓	
		ضَمِيرٌ مُتَّصِلٌ	

---

1. دَقَقْتُ: is اَلْفِعْلُ الْمُضَاعَفُ (دَقَّ يَدُقُّ). It is اَلْفِعْلُ الْمَاضِي and the 'doer' is أَنَا.

2. اَلْبَابَ : is الْمَفْعُولُ, the vowel mark of which is *fatha*.

3. فَفَتَحَتْهُ: In this, فَ is a *'conjunction'* or حَرْفُ الْعَطْفِ. فَتَحَتْ is a 'strong verb' in the past tense and هُ is ضَمِيرٌ مُتَّصِلٌ and الْمَفْعُولُ هُ is joined to the verb as it cannot be written independently after the 'doer'.

4. اَلْخَادِمَةُ: is اَلْفَاعِلُ, the تَشْكِيلٌ of which is *damma*.

INSTRUCTIONS

Grammatically analyse the remaining sentences on this pattern.

136

LESSON SIXTEEN

الْمُثَنَّى وَالْمُثَنَّى الْمُضَافُ
The 'Dual' And The Dual In Construct State
꧁ꕥ꧂

EXAMPLE			
اَلْوَلَدَان	اَلْوَلَدَيْنِ	وَلَدَا مَاجِدٍ	وَلَدَيْ مَاجِدٍ
↓	↓	↓	↓
THE TWO BOYS WITH DAMMA	THE TWO BOYS WITH FATHA AND KASRA	CONSTRUCT STATE WITH DAMMA	CONSTRUCT STATE WITH FATHA AND KASRA

1. Upto this lesson everything that you learnt has been *singular* or مُفْرَدٌ *(mufradun)* like *'a boy or the boy'*.

2. The persons or things in *two* like *'the two boys'* are called the dual or الْمُثَنَّى *(al-muthanna)*.

3. For *damma*: أَلِفٌ and نُونٌ *with kasra* are *suffixed* to اَلْوَلَد to make it 'dual'. For example: اَلْوَلَدُ, 'the boy' and اَلْوَلَدَان: 'the *two* boys'.

4. In اَلْوَلَدَان, the suffix أَلِفٌ is basically the symbol of ضَمَّةٌ. The نُونٌ and its *kasra* need not be taken into account. So اَلْوَلَدَان is 'dual with damma' which you may use as *subject, predicate* or *doer* etc.

5. For both *fatha* and *kasra*: ي and ن with *kasra* are suffixed to الْوَلَد to make it مُثَنَّى. For example: الْوَلَدَيْنَ 'the *two* boys'.

6. In اَلْوَلَدَيْنِ, the suffix ى indicates both كَسْرَةٌ and فَتْحَةٌ. Here too the نُونٌ with its kasra need *not* be taken into account. So

137

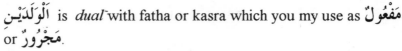

مَفْعُولٌ ٱلْوَلَدَيْـنِ is *dual* with fatha or kasra which you my use as مَجْرُورٌ or.

7. Thus the *dual* is: ٱلْوَلَدَانِ and ٱلْوَلَدَيْنِ.

                ↓   ↓

      AL-WALADAANI   AL-WALADAINI

      IN DAMMA   IN FATHA AND KASRA

8. Memorize both the words and whenever you are asked for the 'dual' in Arabic, always give both these words as :

ٱلْوَلَدَانِ – ٱلْوَلَدَيْنِ   = The two boys.

ٱلْبِنْتَانِ – ٱلْبِنْتَيْنِ   = The two girls.

ٱلْمُدَرِّسَانِ – ٱلْمُدَرِّسَيْنِ   = The two teachers.

ٱلْكِتَابَانِ – ٱلْكِتَابَيْنِ   = The two books.

9. The dual in the *construct state* (ٱلْمُثَنَّى ٱلْمُضَافُ):

When the dual is مُضَافٌ like: 'the two boys *of* Majid', the نُون is *dropped*. Thus it is: وَلَدَا مَاجِدٍ or وَلَدَيْ مَاجِدٍ.

ALSO REMEMBER

10. That if the verb *precedes* the فَاعِلٌ as generally is the case, the verb must be *singular* مُفْرَدٌ e.g.

ذَهَبَ ٱلْوَلَدَانِ   or   ذَهَبَتِ ٱلْبِنْتَانِ

         ↓   ↓

     singular   singular

11. But if the فَاعِلٌ appears *before* the verb, then verb must also be *dual* e.g. ٱلْوَلَدَانِ ذَهَبَا or ٱلْبِنْتَانِ ذَهَبَتَا.

         ↓   ↓

     DUAL   DUAL

12. For *dual subject*, the predicate too *must* be dual with 'alif and nun' e.g.:

ٱلْوَلَدَانِ   ذَاهِبَانِ

 ↓   ↓

مُبْتَدَأٌ   خَبَرٌ

 ↓   ↓

مُثَنَّى   مُثَنَّى

13. For *dual* مَوْصُوفٌ, the صِفَةٌ too must be dual e.g. "The minister attended two important meetings":

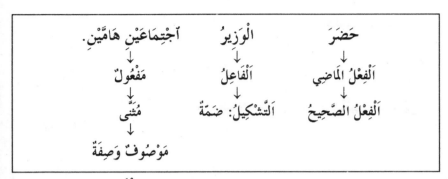

14. For *dual* ضَمِيرٌ مُنْفَصِلٌ (*personal pronoun nominative*):

   (a) *They* (common) : هُمَا e.g. هُمَا وَلَدَانِ or هُمَا بِنْتَانِ.

   (b) *You* (common): أَنْتُمَا e.g. ؟هَلْ أَنْتُمَا تِلْمِيذَانِ or هَلْ أَنْتُمَا تِلْمِيذَتَانِ؟

15. For *dual* ضَمِيرٌ مُتَّصِلٌ (*personal pronoun possessive*):

   (a) *Their* (common): هُمَا e.g.: "*Their* two boys put *their* two books in *their* two bags."

وَضَعَ	وَلَدَاهُمَا	كِتَابَيْهِمَا	فِي	مِحْفَظَتَيْهِمَا.
↓	↓	↓	↓	↓
اَلْفِعْلُ الْمَاضِي	اَلْفَاعِلُ	اَلْمَفْعُولُ	حَرْفُ جَرٍّ	مَجْرُورٌ
↓	↓	↓	↓	↓
اَلْمُفْرَدُ	اَلْمُثَنَّى	اَلْمُثَنَّى الْمُضَافُ	مَبْنِيٌّ عَلَى السُّكُون	اَلْمُثَنَّى الْمُضَافُ
	↓	↓		↓
	ضَمِيرٌ مُتَّصِلٌ	ضَمِيرٌ مُتَّصِلٌ		ضَمِيرٌ مُتَّصِلٌ

   (b) *Your* (common): كُمَا e.g. '*Your* two girls are playing in the garden': بِنْتَاكُمَا لَاعِبَتَانِ فِى الجُنَيْنَةِ.

16. For *dual* اِسْمُ الإِشَارَةِ (*demonstrative pronoun*):

   (a) 'These' (masc.) is: هـذَانِ in case of *damma* and هَذَيْنِ in

139

case of *fatha* and *kasra*. e.g. 'These two boys will read these two books'.

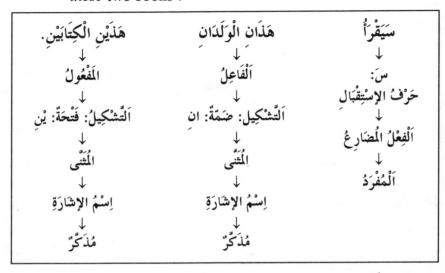

(b) 'These' (*fem.*) is: هَاتَان in case of *damma* and هَاتَيْنِ in case of *fatha* and *kasra*. e.g.

'*These* two girls will read *these* two articles'.

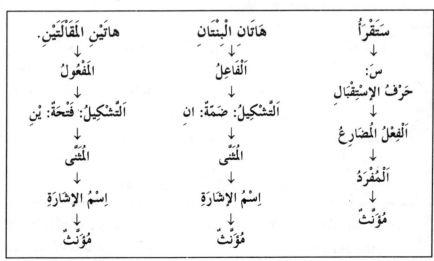

(c) *Those* (masc.): ذَانِكَ for *damma* and ذَيْنِكَ for *fatha* and *kasra*. For example:

For those two boys are two books: لِذَينِكَ الْوَلَدَيْنِ كِتَابَانِ.

(d) Those (fem.): تَانِكَ for *damma* and تَيْنِكَ for *fatha* and *kasra*.

For example: لِتَيْنِكَ الْبِنْتَيْنِ كِتَابَانِ . تَانِكَ بِنْتَانِ

EXERCISE

Grammatically analyse the following sentences :

1. These *two* ministers will attend *two* meetings during the next two days.

سَيَحْضُرُ هَذَانِ الْوَزِيرَانِ اجْتِمَاعَيْنِ خِلَالَ الْيَوْمَيْنِ الْقَادِمَيْنِ.

2. I met the *two* brothers of 'A'isha in the exhibition.

لَقِيتُ أَخَوَيْ عَائِشَةَ فِى الْمَعْرِضِ.

3. The *two* Saudi ministers have gone to London on Monday.

قَدْ ذَهَبَ الْوَزِيرَانِ السُّعُودِيَّانِ إِلَى لَنْدَنَ يَوْمَ الِاثْنَيْنِ.

4. The *two* officials of the Egyptian embassy are absent today.

مُوَظَّفَا السِّفَارَةِ الْمِصْرِيَّةِ غَائِبَانِ الْيَوْمَ.

5. The *two* girls of Majid study in *two* different schools.

تَدْرُسُ بِنْتَا مَاجِدٍ فِى مَدْرَسَتَيْنِ مُخْتَلِفَتَيْنِ.

سَيَحْضُرُ	الْوَزِيرَانِ	اجْتِمَاعَيْنِ	خِلَالَ	الْيَوْمَيْنِ الْقَادِمَيْنِ.
1.	2.	3.	4.	5.
↓	↓	↓	↓	↓
س: حَرْفُ الِاسْتِقْبَال	فَاعِلٌ	مَفْعُولٌ	ظَرْفُ الزَّمَان	مُضَافٌ إِلَيْهِ
↓	↓	↓	↓	↓
فِعْلٌ مُضَارِعٌ	اَلتَّشْكِيلُ: ضَمَّةٌ	اَلتَّشْكِيلُ: فَتْحَةٌ	اَلتَّشْكِيلُ: فَتْحَةٌ	اَلتَّشْكِيلُ: كَسْرَةٌ
↓	↓	↓	↓	↓
مُفْرَدٌ	ان	يْنِ	مُضَافٌ	مَوْصُوفٌ
				↓
				صِفَةٌ

GRAMMATICAL ANALYSIS

141

1. يَحْضُرُ is سَيَحْضُرُ : سَ is *particle of future* like سَوْفَ, and يَحْضُرُ is singular فِعْلٌ مُضَارِعٌ because it is preceding the *dual* فَاعِلٌ.

2. اَلْوَزِيرَان: is فَاعِلٌ the تَشْكِيلٌ of which is *damma* which is expressed by ان in the *dual*.

3. اِجْتِمَاعَيْن: is مَفْعُولٌ the تَشْكِيلٌ of which is *fatha*. It is expressed by يْن in the *dual*.

4. خِلالَ: is ظَرْفُ الزَّمانِ the تَشْكِيلٌ of which is *fatha* and it is مُضَافٌ.

5. اَلْيَوْمَيْنِ الْقَادِمَيْنِ: is مُضَافٌ إِلَيْهِ , the تَشْكِيلٌ of which is *kasra* and which is expressed by يْنِ. It is also صِفَةٌ and مَوْصُوفٌ.

INSTRUCTIONS

Do not proceed to the next lesson before you have well-acquainted yourself with point nos. 10 to 16 which concern the verb, the subject and the predicate, the noun and the adjective, the personal pronouns nominative and possessive, and the demonstrative pronouns in the *dual*.

Grammatically analyse all the remaining sentences.

Write down all the sentences in English given in the exercises of grammar lesson nos. 10 to 15. Translate these 25 sentences into Arabic and later check them with the Arabic text.

الجَمْعُ الْمُكَسَّرُ
The Broken Plural

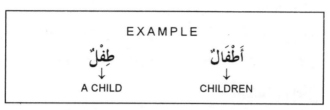

```
                    EXAMPLE
        طِفْلٌ                    أَطْفَالٌ
          ↓                        ↓
       A CHILD                 CHILDREN
```

1. In English, there are *many* ways of converting a singular into a *plural:* 'boy' becomes *boys*, 'man' becomes *men*, 'stadium' becomes *stadia*, 'appendix' becomes *appendices*, 'phenomenon' becomes *phenomena* and 'focus' becomes *foci*.

2. In Arabic too there are many ways of making a noun *plural*. And as all nouns have different plurals they are to be understood and memorized separately.

3. Twelve oft-used أَوْزَانٌ *(awzaanun)* or *patterns* are given below:

    (i) أَفْعَالٌ *(af'aalun)*

    أَسْوَاقٌ : سُوقٌ = *markets*   أَقْلاَمٌ : قَلَمٌ = *pens*

    أَطْفَالٌ : طِفْلٌ = *children*   أَشْجَارٌ : شَجَرٌ = *trees*

    أَسْمَاكٌ : سَمَكٌ = *fish*   أَزْهَارٌ : زَهَرٌ = *flowers*

    أَوْلاَدٌ : وَلَدٌ = *boys*   أَنْهَارٌ : نَهْرٌ = *rivers*

    (ii) فُعُولٌ *(fu'uulun)*

    بُيُوتٌ : بَيْتٌ = *houses*   دُرُوسٌ : دَرْسٌ = *lessons*

    ضُيُوفٌ : ضَيْفٌ = *guests*   هُنُودٌ : هِنْدِيٌّ = *Indians*

    حُقُولٌ : حَقْلٌ = *fields*   جُنُودٌ : جُنْدِيٌّ = *soldiers*

143

رَفٌّ : رُفُوفٌ = almirahs   طَائِرٌ : طُيُورٌ = birds

(iii) فُعُلٌ (fu'ulun)

صَحِيفَةٌ : صُحُفٌ = journals   كِتَابٌ : كُتُبٌ = books

طَرِيقٌ : طُرُقٌ = ways   مَدِينَةٌ : مُدُنٌ = cities

جدارٌ : جُدُرٌ = walls

(iv) فِعَالٌ (fi'aalun)

عُشٌّ : عِشَاشٌ = nests   كَلْبٌ : كِلاَبٌ = dogs

اِمْرَأَةٌ : نِسَاءٌ = women   رَجُلٌ : رِجَالٌ = men

(v) أَفْعُلٌ (af'ulun)

نَهْرٌ : أَنْهُرٌ = rivers   شَهْرٌ : أَشْهُرٌ = months

(vi) فُعَلاَءُ (fu'alaau) diptote.

The plural on this pattern is a *diptote*. If *indefinite*, it will *neither* accept *tanwiin* nor *kasra*.

مُدِيرٌ : مُدَرَاءُ = managers   سَفِيرٌ : سُفَرَاءُ = ambassadors

رَئِيسٌ : رُؤَسَاءُ = presidents   وَزِيرٌ : وُزَرَاءُ = ministers

زَعِيمٌ : زُعَمَاءُ = leaders   عَالِمٌ : عُلَمَاءُ = learned men

(vii) أَفْعِلاَءُ (af'ilaau)

صَدِيقٌ : أَصْدِقاءُ = friends   طَبِيبٌ : أَطِبَّاءُ = doctors

(viii) فُعْلاَنٌ (fu'laanun)

بِلاَدٌ : بُلْدَانٌ = countries

(ix) فَعَالٌ (fa'aalun)

بِنْتٌ : بَنَاتٌ = girls

(x) مَفَاعِلُ (mafaa'ilu) diptote.

The plural on this pattern is a *diptote* (*mamnuu' minas-*

144

sarfi). If *indefinite*, it will *neither* accept *tanwiin* nor *kasra*.

مَوَاقِدُ : مَوْقِدٌ = *stoves*   مَكَاتِبُ : مَكْتَبٌ = *offices*

مَسَاجِدُ : مَسْجِدٌ = *mosques*   مَرَاوِحُ : مِرْوَحَةٌ = *fans*

مَصَانِعُ : مَصْنَعٌ = *factories*   مَدَارِسُ : مَدْرَسَةٌ = *schools*

(xi) فَعْلَى (fa'la)

مَرْضَى : مَرِيضٌ = *patients*

جَرْحَى : جَرِيحٌ = *injured* (persons)

قَتْلَى : قَتِيلٌ = *killed* (persons)

(xii) فَعَالِيلُ (fa'aaliilu) diptote.

The plural on this pattern is a *diptote (mamnu'un minas-sarfi)*. If *indefinite*, it will *neither* accept *tanwiin nor kasra*.

صَنَادِيقُ : صُنْدُوقٌ = *boxes*   كَرَاسِيُّ : كُرْسِيٌّ = *chairs*

عَصَافِيرُ : عُصْفُورٌ = *sparrows*   تَلَامِيذُ : تِلْمِيذٌ = *students*

سَكَاكِينُ : سِكِّينٌ = *knives*   دَكَاكِينُ : دُكَّانٌ = *shops*

4. Remember that these patterns are just those on which most plurals are formed. You should expect *more* patterns. Plurals of nouns are to be learnt individually as there is *no* fixed rule for constructing them.

5. This plural is called the *broken* plural اَلْجَمْعُ الْمُكَسَّرُ because it is formed only after *breaking up the singular*. As you notice, for سُفَرَاءُ the singular سَفِيرٌ was broken up in order to eliminate its third letter ى and to insert اَلِفٌ and هَمْزَةٌ in the end. Or like the singular: اِمْرَأَةٌ (a woman) which underwent a total change *losing all* the original letters of the singular while being transformed into plural: نِسَاءٌ (*women*).

6. That the rules for *sensible* plural (لِلْعَـاقِل for *humans*) differ from those for *insensible* plural (لِغَيْرِ الْعَـاقِل) for *animals or objects* etc.

7. Thus if the plural is for the *sensible*: لِلْعَاقِل:

   (a) Plural subject's *predicate* will also be plural, e.g. the students are bright: اَلتَّلاَمِيذُ أَذْكِيَاءُ.

   (b) If the verb *precedes* the فَاعِلٌ, it will remain *singular*, e.g. The students *went*: ذَهَبَ التَّلاَمِيذُ.

   (c) If the فَاعِلٌ *precedes the verb,* it too will be in plural, e.g. The students *went*: اَلتَّلاَمِيذُ ذَهَبُوا.

   (d) The plural مَوْصُوفٌ will have a plural صِفَةٌ, e.g. The *bright* students succeeded: نَجَحَ التَّلاَمِيذُ الأَذْكِيَاءُ.

8. If the plural is for the *insensible* (لِغَيْرِ الْعَاقِل) i.e., animals or objects:

   (a) Then the plural *subject* will have *singular feminine predicate* e.g. The *offices* are far:

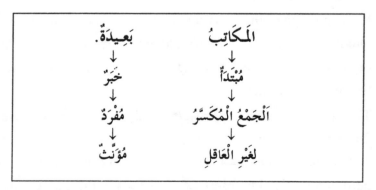

   (b) And for insensible *plural doer,* the verb will be *singular feminine* e.g. The trees *grew*:

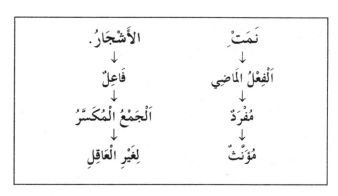

(c) The صِفَة for *insensible plural* is *singular feminine* e.g. The *big* houses are expensive:

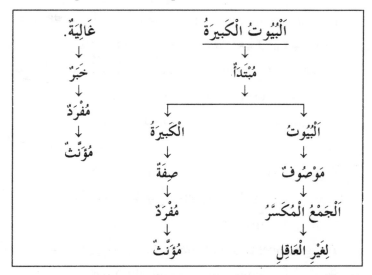

9. The plural for *'personal pronoun nominative'*: ضَمِيرٌ مُنْفَصِلٌ is:

(a) هِيَ : 'They' (insensible) e.g.

They are birds: هِيَ طُيُورٌ

(b) هُمْ : 'They' (masc.) (sensible) e.g.

They are boys : هُمْ أَوْلَادٌ.

(c) هُنَّ : 'They' (fem.) (sensible) e.g.

They are girls: هُنَّ بَنَاتٌ.

(d) أَنْتُمْ : 'You' (masc.) (sensible) e. g.

You are men: أَنْتُمْ رِجَالٌ.

(e) أَنْتُنَّ : 'You' (fem.) (sensible) e. g.

You are girls: أَنْتُنَّ بَنَاتٌ.

(f) نَحْنُ : 'We' (common) e.g.

We are boys : نَحْنُ أَوْلَادٌ.

We are girls : نَحْنُ بَنَاتٌ.

10. The plural for *'personal pronoun possessive'*: ضَمِيرٌ مُتَّصِلٌ is:

(a) *Suffix* هَا: *'their'* (insensible) e.g.

The birds live in *their* nests : تَعِيشُ الطُّيُورُ فِى عِشَاشِهَا

(b) *Suffix* هُمْ and هِمْ: *'their'* (masc.) (sensible) e.g.

The students opened *their* books : فَتَحَ التَّلَامِيذُ كُتُبَهُمْ

Suffix هِمْ is used in case of *kasra* e.g.

The students went back to *their* houses :

عَادَ التَّلَامِيذُ إِلَى بُيُوتِهِمْ.

(c) *Suffix* هُنَّ and هِنَّ : *'their'* (fem.) (sensible) e.g.

The girls read *their* books : قَرَأَتِ الْبَنَاتُ كُتُبَهُنَّ

Suffix هِنَّ is used in case of *kasra* e.g.

The girls went to *their* homes : ذَهَبَتِ الْبَنَاتُ إِلَى بُيُوتِهِنَّ

(d) *Suffix* كُمْ : *'your'* (masc.) (sensible) e.g.

O' boys, open *your* books: يَا أَوْلَادُ، اِفْتَحُوا كُتُبَكُمْ

(e) Suffix كُنَّ : *'your'* (fem.) (sensible) e.g.

O'girls, read *your* lessons: يَا بَنَاتُ، اِقْرَأْنَ دُرُوسَكُنَّ

(f) Suffix نا : *'our'* (common) e.g.

We will return to *our* homes in the evening:

سَنَعُودُ إِلَى بُيُوتِنَا فِي الْمَسَاءِ.

11. The plural for *'the demonstrative pronoun'*: اِسْمُ الْإِشَارَةِ is:

(a) هَذِهِ (singular feminine) for *'these'* (insensible) e.g.

These are books: هذِهِ كُتُبٌ.

تِلْكَ (singular feminine) for *'those'* (insensible) e.g.

Those are birds: تِلْكَ طُيُورٌ.

(b) هَؤُلاَءِ (*haa'ulaa'i*) *these* (common) (sensible) e.g.

These are boys/girls : هَؤُلاَءِ أَوْلادٌ – هَؤُلاَءِ بَنَاتٌ

(c) أُولَئِكَ (*ulaa'ika*) *those* (common) (sensible) e.g.

Those are boys/girls. أُولَئِكَ أَوْلادٌ – أُولَئِكَ بَنَاتٌ

EXERCISE

Grammatically analyse the following sentences :

1. The government offices are closed on Sunday.

اَلْمَكَاتِبُ الْحُكُومِيَّةُ مُغْلَقَةٌ يَوْمَ الأَحَدِ.

2. Those women do not work in government offices.

لا تَعْمَلُ أُولَئِكَ النِّسَاءُ فى مَكَاتِبَ حُكُومِيَّةٍ.

أَوْ : أُولَئِكَ النِّسَاءُ لا يَعْمَلْنَ فى مَكَاتِبَ حُكُومِيَّةٍ.

3. Please put these new books in the racks.

مِنْ فَضْلِكَ ، ضَعْ هَذِهِ الْكُتُبَ الْجَدِيدَةَ فِي الرُّفُوفِ.

4. We have studied many new lessons in Arabic .

قَدْ دَرَسْنَا دُرُوساً جَدِيدَةً كَثِيرَةً فِي الْعَرَبِيَّةِ.

5. These men and women work in those small factories.

يَعْمَلُ هَؤُلاَءِ الرِّجَالُ والنِّسَاءُ فى تِلْكَ الْمَصَانِعِ الصَّغِيرَةِ.

GRAMMATICAL ANALYSIS

لَا	تَعْمَلُ	أُولَئِكَ	النِّسَاءُ	فِي	مَكَاتِبَ	حُكُومِيَّةٍ.
1	2	3	4	5	6	7
↓	↓	↓	↓	↓	↓	↓
حَرْفُ	اَلْفِعْلُ	اِسْمُ	اَلْفَاعِلُ	حَرْفُ	مَجْرُورٌ	صِفَةٌ
النَّفْي	الْمُضَارِعُ	الإشَارَة	↓	الْجَرِّ	↓	↓
↓	↓	↓	اَلتَّشْكِيلُ:	↓	مَمْنُوعٌ مِنَ	مُفْرَدٌ
مَبْنِيٌّ عَلَى	مُفْرَدٌ	لِلْجَمْعِ	ضَمَّةٌ	مَبْنِيٌّ	الصَّرْفِ	↓
السُّكُون		لِلْعَاقِل	↓		↓	مُؤَنَّثٌ
			اَلْجَمْعُ		مَوْصُوفٌ	
			الْمُكَسَّرُ		↓	
					اَلْجَمْعُ الْمُكَسَّرُ	

1. لَا : is called 'the particle of negation' or حَرْفُ النَّفِي.

2. تَعْمَلُ : is اَلْفِعْلُ الْمُضَارِعُ. As it *precedes* the plural, it has to be *singular*.

3. أُولَئِكَ : is اِسْمُ الإشَارَةِ to refer to 'sensible' plural.

4. النِّسَاءُ : is اَلْفَاعِلُ and its vowel point is *damma*. It is a 'broken plural' اَلْجَمْعُ الْمُكَسَّرُ.

5. فِي : is حَرْفُ الْجَرِّ and it is مَبْنِيٌّ (indeclinable).

6. مَكَاتِبَ : is مَجْرُورٌ and a *diptote* plural which means that if *indefinite* it can *neither* accept kasra *nor* nunation. In case of kasra, such diptote is given *fatha*. It is also مَوْصُوفٌ 'the noun qualified'.

7. حُكُومِيَّةٍ : is صِفَةٌ of an 'insensible' plural, therefore it is 'singular feminine'.

ALSO REMEMBER

That the above sentence can be written differently, *without* any change in its meaning, but with a different grammatical structure:

150

4	3	2	1
مَكَاتِبَ حَكُومِيَّةٍ.	فِي	لَا يَعْمَلْنَ	أُولَئِكَ النِّسَاءُ
↓	↓	↓	↓
مَجْرُورٌ	حَرْفُ جَرٍّ	خَبَرٌ	مُبْتَدَأٌ
↓	↓	↓	↓
مَوْصُوفٌ	مَبْنِيٌّ عَلَى السُّكُونِ	جُمْلَةٌ فِعْلِيَّةٌ	اَلتَّشْكِيلُ: ضَمَّةٌ
↓		↓	↓
جَمْعٌ		لَا: حَرْفُ النَّفْيِ	اِسْمُ الإِشَارَةِ
↓			↓
مَمْنُوعٌ مِنَ الصَّرْفِ			لِلْعَاقِلِ
↓			↓
صِفَةٌ			اَلْمُشَارُ إِلَيْهِ

1. أُولَئِكَ النِّسَاءُ : مُبْتَدَأٌ and *not* فَاعِلٌ. You have learnt in the first lesson on 'verb' (lesson number: 7) that it is *better* if the verb precedes the *doer*; but even if the 'doer' precedes the verb, it is correct, and as this فَاعِلٌ precedes the verb, it is to be called the 'subject'.

2. لَا يَعْمَلْنَ : is خَبَرٌ (predicate) which consists of حَرْفُ النَّفْيِ and a present tense verb that *agrees* with the مُبْتَدَأٌ in being plural (unlike *singular* تَعْمَلُ in the previous sentence).

3. فِي : is a preposition, the last letter of which is invariably سَاكِنٌ.

4. مَكَاتِبَ حُكُومِيَّةٍ: is مَجْرُورٌ and مَوْصُوفٌ and صِفَةٌ. The مَوْصُوفٌ (مَكَاتِبَ) is a diptote which, *if indefinite*, neither accepts كَسْرَةٌ nor تَنْوِينٌ and in such cases it is given *fatha*. The صِفَةٌ, however, is *not* a diptote and thus it *accepts* both the kasra and the nunation. As the مَوْصُوفٌ is *insensible* plural, the صِفَةٌ is *singular feminine*.

151

INSTRUCTIONS

Grammatically analyse all the sentences. The mastering of the Arabic grammar largely depends on your capacity to analyse the sentences in Arabic beside memorizing the rules.

Note down in your notebook the thirty sentences which you found in the exercises of the last six grammar lessons. Translate them into Arabic and then check them against the Arabic text.

الجَمْعُ المُذَكَّرُ السَّالِمُ والمُضَافُ

The Sound Masculine Plural and Its Form In Construct State

> ❧❦❧

EXAMPLES			
المُدَرِّسُونَ	المُدَرِّسِينَ	مُدَرِّسُو الجَامِعَةِ	مُدَرِّسِي الجَامِعَةِ
↓	↓	↓	↓
SOUND MASC.	SOUND MASC.	المُضَافُ	المُضَافُ
PLURAL WITH	PLURAL WITH	↓	↓
DAMMA	FATHA AND	WITH	WITH FATHA
	KASRA	DAMMA	AND KASRA

1. The plural which you studied in the last lesson was the *broken* plural. In it you noticed that the singular noun was broken up and some letter or letters were either *deleted or added*.

2. In Arabic, there are such *masculine nouns* too in which only *two* specific letters are *suffixed* in order to turn them into plural. As *no* part of the singular is *broken up,* such plurals are called : *'The sound masculine plurals'*.

3. In Arabic, the sound masculine plural is called الجَمْعُ المُذَكَّرُ السَّالِمُ (*al-jam'ul-mudhakkarus-saalimu*).

4. For *damma:*

    واو and نُونٌ with *fatha* are *suffixed* to the masculine singular. Here واو symbolizes *damma,* the نُونٌ and its فَتْحَةٌ need *not* be taken into consideration.

    Thus :

مُوَظَّفٌ becomes : مُوَظَّفُونَ : officers

فَلَّاحٌ becomes : فَلَّاحُونَ : farmers

مُدَرِّسٌ becomes : مُدَرِّسُونَ : teachers

The usage:

الْمُدَرِّسُونَ مَشْغُولُونَ.　　　جَاءَ الْمُوَظَّفُونَ.

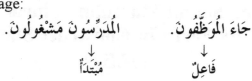

5. For *fatha* and *kasra*:

ي and نُونْ with *fatha* are *suffixed* to express both *fatha* and *kasra*. Here ي symbolizes *fatha* or *kasra*. The نُونْ and its *fatha* need *not* be taken into consideration.

Thus :

مُوَظَّفٌ becomes : مُوَظَّفِينَ

فَلَّاحٌ becomes : فَلَّاحِينَ

مُدَرِّسٌ becomes : مُدَرِّسِينَ

The usage :

لَقِيتُ مُوَظَّفِينَ. ذَهَبَ الْفَلَّاحُونَ مَعَ الْمُوَظَّفِينَ.

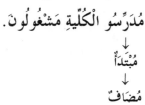

6. The sound masculine plural in *construct state*:

In case مُدَرِّسُونَ and مُدَرِّسِينَ happen to be مُضَافٌ, their نُونْ is invariably *deleted*.

For example:

The teachers *of* the college are busy:

مُدَرِّسُو الْكُلِّيةِ مَشْغُولُونَ.

Les-13.d

The officer went with the farmers *of* the village:

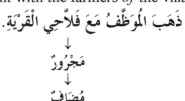

7. Other than keen observation and practice, there is *no* easy way of knowing which nouns belong to 'broken plural' category and those which belong to الجَمْعُ الْمُذَكَّرُ السَّالِمُ. As each noun has a *different* plural, all the Arabic dictionaries first specify this aspect.

8. Some commonly used nouns with plurals on this pattern are being identified. Repeat them loudly:

(1)	مُسَافِرٌ : traveller		(9)	مُهَنْدِسٌ : engineer	
(2)	مُحَاضِرٌ : lecturer		(10)	فَرَّاشٌ : peon	
(3)	إِسْرَائِيلِيٌّ : Israeli		(11)	حَمَّالٌ : porter	
(4)	أَمْرِيكِيٌّ : American		(12)	إِرْهَابِيٌّ : terrorist	
(5)	مُوَاطِنٌ : citizen		(13)	سِيَاسِيٌّ : politician	
(6)	دِبْلُومَاسِيٌّ : diplomat		(14)	مُقَاتِلٌ : fighter	
(7)	بَاكِسْتَانِيٌّ : Pakistani		(15)	فِلَسْطِينِيٌّ : Palestinian	
(8)	سَائِقٌ : driver		(16)	عَسْكَرِيٌّ : militaryman	

EXERCISE

Grammatically analyse the following sentences:

1. These American engineers are very hard working.

هَؤُلاَءِ الْمُهَنْدِسُونَ الأَمْرِيكِيُونَ مُجْتَهِدُونَ جِدّاً.

2. The President called the Iranian diplomats for an important meeting.

دَعَا الرَّئِيسُ الدِّبْلُومَاسِيِّينَ الإِيرَانِيِّينَ لِاجْتِمَاعٍ هَامٍّ.

3. The lecturers of the university returned to their homes in the evening.

رَجَعَ مُحَاضِرُو الْجَامِعَةِ إِلَى بُيُوتِهِمْ مَسَاءً.

4. The armymen killed many terrorists in the mountains.

قَتَلَ الْعَسْكَرِيُّونَ إِرْهَابِيِّينَ كَثِيرِينَ فِى الْجِبَالِ.

5. The Israelis launched a big attack on the Palestinian fighters.

شَنَّ الْإِسْرَائِيلِيُّونَ هُجُوماً كَبِيراً عَلَى الْمُقَاتِلِينَ الْفِلَسْطِينِيِّينَ.

GRAMMATICAL ANALYSIS

شَنَّ   الْإِسْرَائِيلِيُّونَ   هُجُوماً كَبِيراً   عَلَى   الْمُقَاتِلِينَ الْفِلَسْطِينِيِّينَ.

1   2   3   4   5

↓   ↓   ↓   ↓   ↓

اَلْفِعْلُ   اَلْفَاعِلُ   اَلْمَفْعُولُ   حَرْفُ جَرٍّ   مَجْرُورٌ

اَلْمُضَاعَفُ   ↓   ↓   ↓

↓   اَلتَّشْكِيلُ:   اَلْمَوْصُوفُ   اَلْمُقَاتِلِينَ: مَوْصُوفٌ

اَلْمُفْرَدُ   ضَمَّةٌ   ↓   ↓

   ↓   الصِّفَةُ   الْفِلَسْطِينِيِّينَ: صِفَةٌ

اَلْجَمْعُ الْمُذَكَّرُ   ↓

السَّالِمُ   لِلْعَاقِلِ

1. شَنَّ : is the *doubled* verb: اَلْفِعْلُ الْمُضَاعَفُ in the past tense. It is singular because it *precedes* the plural 'doer': الْإِسْرَائِيلِيُّونَ.

2. الْإِسْرَائِيلِيُّونَ : is the 'doer': اَلْفَاعِلُ, the تَشْكِيلٌ of which is *damma*. As it is the 'sound masculine plural,' the *damma* is expressed by ونَ.

3. هُجُوماً كَبِيراً : is the 'object' or الْمَفْعُولُ, the case ending of which is *fatha*. It is also صِفَةٌ and مَوْصُوفٌ.

156

4. عَلَى : is a 'preposition'.

5. الْمُقَاتِلِينَ الْفِلَسْطِينِيِّينَ both are : الْمُقَاتِلِينَ is مَوْصُوفٌ مَجْرُورٌ in which the kasra is expressed by ين : اَلْجَمْعُ الْمُذَكَّرُ السَّالِمُ. And اَلْفِلَسْطِينِيِّينَ : is صِفَـــةٌ which *agrees* with the مَوْصُوفٌ in being plural.

	MORE ANALYSIS				
مَسَاءً	بُيُوتِهِمْ	إِلَى	الْجَامِعَةِ	مُحَاضِرُو	رَجَعَ
↓	↓	↓	↓	↓	↓
ظَرْفُ الزَّمَانِ	اَلْمَجْرُورُ	حَرْفُ جَرٍّ	الْمُضَافُ	اَلْفَاعِلُ	اَلْفِعْلُ
			إِلَيْهِ	↓	الْمَاضِي
اَلتَّشْكِيلُ: اَلْجَمْعُ الْمُكَسَّرُ	مَبْنِيٌّ عَلَى	↓	اَلْجَمْعُ الْمُذَكَّرُ	↓
فَتْحَةٌ	↓	السُّكُونِ	الْمَعْرِفَةُ	السَّالِمُ	اَلْفِعْلُ
	ضَمِيرٌ			↓	الصَّحِيحُ
	مُتَّصِلٌ: هِمْ			الْمُضَافُ	

157

الجَمْعُ المُؤَنَّثُ السَّالِمُ
The Sound Feminine Plural

꿎꿎ꕥ꿎꿎

EXAMPLE

مُدَرِّسَاتٌ	مُدَرِّسَاتٍ
↓	↓
SOUND FEMININE PLURAL WITH DAMMA	SOUND FEMININE PLURAL WITH FATHA AND KASRA

---

1. The third and the last category of plural in Arabic is called the *sound feminine plural*.

2. The 'sound feminine plural' is called: اَلجَمْعُ المُؤَنَّثُ السَّالِمُ in Arabic.

3. This plural is named the '*sound feminine* plural' because the singular noun, generally a feminine one, is *suffixed* with two letters أَلِفٌ and تَاءٌ for making it a plural. In other words, the singular (unlike the broken plural) does not undergo any change in the form of *deletion* or *addition*. Hence its name: 'the *sound* feminine plural'.

4. Predominantly the singulars for this plural are *feminine*, that is with the round ة *suffixed* to them. Only a few are masculine.

5. In case of *damma*:

    'أَلِفٌ' and 'تَاءٌ' with *damma* are *suffixed* to the singular after *deleting* the 'round ta' (ة) Thus:

    مُدَرِّسَةٌ becomes مُدَرِّسَاتٌ (lady teachers).

اَلْمُدَرِّسَةُ becomes اَلْمُدَرِّسَاتُ (the lady teachers).

For example :

The *lady teachers* are hardworking: اَلْمُدَرِّسَاتُ مُجْتَهِدَاتٌ.

6. In case of *fatha* and *kasra*:

'alif and taa' with *kasra* are *suffixed* to the singular. Thus:

سَيَّارَةً and سَيَّارَةٍ *both* become : سَيَّارَاتٍ.

اَلْمُدَرِّسَةَ and اَلْمُدَرِّسَةِ both become: اَلْمُدَرِّسَاتِ.

For example :

I saw new *cars :* رَأَيْتُ سَيَّارَاتٍ جَدِيدَةً.

The students went with *the lady teachers:*

ذَهَبَ التَّلَامِيذُ مَعَ الْمُدَرِّسَاتِ.

7. Unlike the sound masculine plural discussed earlier, in case of construct state *nothing* is deleted.

8. Thus if you are asked for the plural of such noun, give both the forms : الْمُدَرِّسَاتِ and الْمُدَرِّسَاتُ.

9. The commonly used singulars, the plural of which appear as sound feminine plural, are being identified below. Read them aloud. And do note that barring a few, all have the feminine round ة suffixed to them.

(1)	مَكْتَبَةٌ : مَكْتَبَاتٌ	= libraries
(2)	طَائِرَةٌ : طَائِرَاتٌ	= aeroplanes
(3)	صَفْحَةٌ : صَفَحَاتٌ	= pages
(4)	كُلِّيَّةٌ : كُلِّيَّاتٌ	= colleges
(5)	ثَلَّاجَةٌ : ثَلَّاجَاتٌ	= refrigerators
(6)	سَاعَةٌ : سَاعَاتٌ	= watches
(7)	جَامِعَةٌ : جَامِعَاتٌ	= universities
(8)	صَيْدَلِيَّةٌ : صَيْدَلِيَّاتٌ	= chemists' shops

159

(9) فَلَّاحَاتٌ : فَلَّاحَةٌ	= lady farmers
(10) كُرَّاسَاتٌ : كُرَّاسَةٌ	= notebooks
(11) طِفْلَاتٌ : طِفْلَةٌ	= children
(12) مَجَلَّاتٌ : مَجَلَّةٌ	= magazines
(13) زُجَاجَاتٌ : زُجَاجَةٌ	= bottles
(14) مُمَرِّضَاتٌ : مُمَرِّضَةٌ	= nurses
(15) عُطْلَاتٌ : عُطْلَةٌ	= holidays

Those with singular as *masculine:*

(16) بَيَانَاتٌ : بَيَانٌ	= statements
(17) خِطَابَاتٌ : خِطَابٌ	= letters
(18) مُسْتَشْفَيَاتٌ : مُسْتَشْفًى	= hospitals

EXERCISE

Grammatically analyse the following sentences:

1. I read many English magazines last month:

قَرَأْتُ مَجَلَّاتٍ إِنْجِلِيزِيَّةً كَثِيرَةً اَلشَّهْرَ اَلْمَاضِيَ.

2. These nurses are working in those hospitals:

هَؤُلَاءِ الْمُمَرِّضَاتُ عَامِلَاتٌ فِي تِلْكَ الْمُسْتَشْفَيَاتِ.

3. The students go to different libraries in the evening:

يَذْهَبُ التَّلَامِيذُ إِلَى مَكْتَبَاتٍ مُخْتَلِفَةٍ مَسَاءً.

4. The schools and colleges are closed during holidays:

الْمَدَارِسُ وَالْكُلِّيَاتُ مُغْلَقَةٌ خِلَالَ عُطْلَاتٍ.

5. The chemists shops are far from hospitals in this city:

اَلصَّيْدَلِيَّاتُ بَعِيدَةٌ مِنْ مُسْتَشْفَيَاتٍ فِي هَذِهِ الْمَدِينَةِ.

٥	٤	٣	٢	١
اَلشَّهْرَ المَاضِيَ.	كَثِيرَةً	اِنْجليزِيَّةٍ	مَجَلَّاتٍ	قَرَأْتُ
↓	↓	↓	↓	↓
ظَرْفُ الزَّمَان	اَلصِّفَةُ	اَلصِّفَةُ	اَلْمَفْعُولُ	اَلْفِعْلُ المَاضِي
↓	↓	↓	↓	↓
اَلتَّشْكِيلُ: فَتْحَة	اَلْمُفْرَدُ	اَلْمُفْرَدُ	اَلْجَمْعُ	اَلْفِعْلُ
↓	↓	↓	المُؤَنَّثُ	الصَّحِيحُ
المَوْصُوفُ	المُؤَنَّثُ	المُؤَنَّثُ	السَّالِمُ	↓
↓	↓	↓		اَلْفَاعِلُ: أَنَا
الصِّفَةُ	النَّكِرَةُ	النَّكِرَةُ		

1. قَرَأْتُ = is a past tense 'strong verb' (اَلْفِعْلُ الصَّحِيحُ) and the 'doer' is an *implicit* أَنَا.

2. مَجَلَّاتٍ = is مَفْعُولٌ the vowel mark of which is *fatha*. It is also the 'sound feminine plural' with اَلِف and تْ. This suffix gets *kasra* in case of *fatha*. It is also مَوْصُوفٌ , the *'noun qualified'*.

3. اِنْجليزِيَّةٍ = is صِفَةٌ of مَجَلَّاتٍ. It is feminine and indefinite. *Unlike* مَجَلَّاتٍ, it carries *fatha*.

4. كَثِيرَةً = is the *second* صِفَةٌ for مَجَلَّاتٍ. It too is feminine and indefinite like the مَوْصُوفٌ.

5. اَلشَّهْرَ المَاضِيَ = is the *adverb of time* or ظَرْفُ الزَّمَان the تَشْكِيلٌ of which is *fatha* and it consists of a مَوْصُوفٌ and a صِفَةٌ.

اَلْفِعْلُ الْمَجْهُولُ
The Passive Verb
❧❦❧

		EXAMPLE		
The	**man**	**was killed.**	الرَّجُلُ	قُتِلَ
		↓	↓	↓
		THE PASSIVE	نَائِبُ	اَلْفِعْلُ
		VERB	اَلْفَاعِلِ	الْمَجْهُولُ

1. In the sentence: "The man killed" : قَتَلَ الرَّجُلُ, the verb قَتَلَ is an "active verb" called اَلْفِعْلُ الْمَعْرُوفُ (al-fi'lul-ma'ruufu).

2. In the above example: was killed is a "passive verb" called اَلْفِعْلُ الْمَجْهُولُ (al-fi'lul-majhuulu).

3. Here, 'the man' is called نَائِبُ الْفَاعِلِ (naa'ibul-faa'ili).

4. The تَشْكِيلٌ of نَائِبُ الْفَاعِلِ is damma.

5. For the passive in الْمَاضِي two changes are made in an 'active verb' قَتَلَ :

   (1) Its first letter is given ضَمَّةٌ, and

   (2) the penultimate letter is given كَسْرَةٌ. Thus قُتِلَ : (he was killed).

6. For the passive in الْمُضَارِعُ, two changes are made in the 'active verb' يَقْتُلُ :

   (1) The first letter is given ضَمَّةٌ and

   (2) The penultimate letter is given فَتْحَةٌ. Thus يُقْتَلُ : (he is killed).

7. There is *no* word here for : *is or was or were.*

8. Thus, the above sentence is translated as: قُتِلَ الرَّجُلُ (The man was killed).

9. That *only a transitive* verb (اَلْفِعْلُ الْمُتَعَدِّي) or one accepting a مَفْعُولٌ like قَتَلَ, فَتَحَ or أَخَذَ etc. can be converted into a فِعْلٌ مَجْهُولٌ.

10. Thus an intransitive verb (اَلْفِعْلُ اللَّازِمُ) like ذَهَبَ is *never* used as ذُهِبَ or يُذْهَبُ.

11. اَلْمُضَارِعُ in يُقْتَلُ and اَلْمَاضِي in قُتِلَ have the same prefixes and suffixes of an 'active verb' in their conjugations e.g.

اَلْمَاضِي الْمَجْهُولُ :

قُتِلْنَ	قُتِلَتَا	قُتِلَتْ	قُتِلُوا	قُتِلَا	قُتِلَ
قُتِلْتُنَّ	قُتِلْتُمَا	قُتِلْتِ	قُتِلْتُمْ	قُتِلْتُمَا	قُتِلْتَ
				قُتِلْنَا	قُتِلْتُ

اَلْمُضَارِعُ الْمَجْهُولُ :

يُقْتَلْنَ	تُقْتَلَانِ	تُقْتَلُ	يُقْتَلُونَ	يُقْتَلَانِ	يُقْتَلُ
تُقْتَلْنَ	تُقْتَلَانِ	تُقْتَلِينَ	تُقْتَلُونَ	تُقْتَلَانِ	تُقْتَلُ
				نُقْتَلُ	أُقْتَلُ

12. To negate مَجْهُولٌ :

   (a) مَا is used in مَاضٍ as in : مَا قُتِلَ الرَّجُلُ *(the man was not killed)* and

   (b) لاَ is used in مُضَارِعٌ as in : لاَ يُفْتَحُ الْمَصْرَفُ فِي الْمَسَاءِ (The bank *is not opened* in the evening.)

13. The *weak* verbs in the 'passive' are as follows :

163

(1)	قَالَ يَقُولُ	is :	قِيلَ يُقَالُ	(was/is said).
(2)	بَاعَ يَبِيعُ	is :	بِيعَ يُبَاعُ	(was/is sold).
(3)	نَالَ يَنَالُ	is :	نِيلَ يُنَالُ	(was/is achieved).
(4)	دَعَا يَدْعُو	is :	دُعِيَ يُدْعَى	(was/is called).
(5)	طَوَى يَطْوِي	is :	طُوِيَ يُطْوَى	(was/is folded).
(6)	وَجَدَ يَجِدُ	is :	وُجِدَ يُوجَدُ	(was/is found).

EXERCISE

Grammatically analyse the following sentences:

1. The gate of the embassy *is opened* every morning.

يُفْتَحُ بَابُ السِّفَارَةِ كُلَّ صَبَاحٍ.

2. This house *was sold* last month. بِيعَ هَذَا الْبَيْتُ الشَّهْرَ الْمَاضِيَ.

3. The oil *is found* in the sea. يُوجَدُ النَّفْطُ فِي الْبَحْرِ.

4. His name *was not written* on the door. مَا كُتِبَ اسْمُهُ عَلَى الْبَابِ.

5. That office *is not opened* every day. لَا يُفْتَحُ ذَلِكَ الْمَكْتَبُ كُلَّ يَوْمٍ.

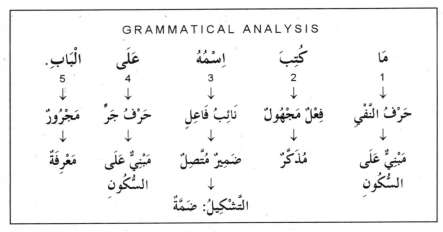

الْبَابِ.	عَلَى	اسْمُهُ	كُتِبَ	مَا
5	4	3	2	1
↓	↓	↓	↓	↓
مَجْرُورٌ	حَرْفُ جَرٍّ	نَائِبُ فَاعِلٍ	فِعْلٌ مَجْهُولٌ	حَرْفُ النَّفْيِ
↓	↓	↓	↓	↓
مَعْرِفَةٌ	مَبْنِيٌّ عَلَى السُّكُونِ	ضَمِيرٌ مُتَّصِلٌ	مُذَكَّرٌ	مَبْنِيٌّ عَلَى السُّكُونِ
		↓		
		التَّشْكِيلُ: ضَمَّةٌ		

GRAMMATICAL ANALYSIS

1. مَا: is a negative particle or حَرْفُ النَّفْيِ. It is an indeclinable word: مَبْنِيٌّ.

2. كُتِبَ : is اَلْفِعْلُ الصَّحِيحُ, 'the strong verb'. It is مَجْهُولٌ in the past tense.

3. اِسْمُهُ : is نَائِبُ اَلْفَاعِلِ and its تَشْكِيلٌ is ضَمَّةٌ. It is مُذَكَّرٌ and ه is ضَمِيرٌ مُتَّصِلٌ.

4. عَلَى : is a preposition and مَبْنِيٌّ عَلَى السُّكُونِ. Its case ending *never* changes.

5. الْبَابِ : is مَجْرُورٌ or 'the noun governed by a preposition'. The *alif* in the 'definite article' is هَمْزَةُ الوَصْلِ meaning the '*joining hamza*'. It is *not* pronounced. Thus: *'ala'l-baabi.*

INDEX

A

166

Amr	أَمْر	Lesson 9	Point 1
Amsi	أَمْس	Lesson 13	Point 6
'An	عَنْ	Lesson 2	Point 7
Anta	أَنْتَ	Lesson 4	Point 3
Anti	أَنْتِ	Lesson 4	Point 3
Antum	أَنْتُمْ	Lesson 17	Point 9
Antumaa	أَنْتُمَا	Lesson 16	Point 14
Antunna	أَنْتُنَّ	Lesson 17	Point 9
Ash-shaklu	الشَّكْلُ	Introduction	Point 7
Asmaa ush-shuhuuri	أَسْمَاءُ الشُّهُورِ	Lesson 11	Point 30
'Atf (huruuful-'atf)	عَطْف	Lesson 11	Point 7
Aw	أَوْ	Lesson 11	Point 7
Awzaan jam'in mukassarin			
	أَوْزَانُ جَمْعٍ مُكَسَّرٍ	Lesson 17	Point 3
Ayyatu	أَيَّةُ	Lesson 11	Point 11
Ayyatuhaa	أَيَّتُهَا	Lesson 11	Point 14
Ayyu	أَيُّ	Lesson 11	Point 11
Ayyuhaa	أَيُّهَا	Lesson 11	Point 14

B

Baa'a -yabii'u	بَاعَ يَبِيعُ	Lesson 12-B	
B'ada	بَعْدَ	Lesson 13	Point 7
Baina	بَيْنَ	Lesson 14	Point 6
Bal	بَلْ	Lesson 11	Point 7
Bi	بِ	Lesson 2	Point 7
Bi-jiwaari	بجوَار	Lesson 14	Point 6
Broken plural	الْجَمْعُ الْمُكَسَّرُ	Lesson 17	
But	لكِنْ	Lesson 11	Point 7

167

C

D

E

169

F

171

Haati	هَاتِ	Lesson 9	Point 10
Hatta (conjunction)	حَتَّى	Lesson 11	Point 7
Hatta (preposition)	حَتَّى	Lesson 2	Point 7
Have	عِنْدَ	Lesson 11	Point 25
Hiya	هِيَ	Lesson 4	Point 3
Hu	ه	Lesson 4	Point 7
Hum	هُمْ	Lesson 17	Point 10
Humaa	هُمَا	Lesson 16	P 14,15
Hunaa	هُنَا	Lesson 14	Point 7
Hunaaka	هُنَاكَ	Lesson 14	Point 7
Hunna	هُنَّ	Lesson 17	Point 10
Huwa	هُوَ	Lesson 4	Point 3

I

Ii (damiirun muttasilun)	ي	Lesson 4	Point 7:5
Ijtimaa' us-saakinaini	اِجْتِمَاعُ السَّاكِنَيْن	Lesson 12	Point 7
Ilaa	إِلَى	Lesson 2	Point 7
Imperative verb	فِعْلُ الأَمْرِ	Lesson 9	
'Inda	عِنْدَ	Lesson 11	Point 25
Indeclinable noun	مَبْنِيٌّ	Lesson 11	Point 4
Indefinite noun	نَكِرَةٌ	Lesson 11	Point 1
Infinitive	مَصْدَرٌ	Lesson 11	Point 27
Insensible plural	اَلْجَمْعُ لِغَيْرِ عَاقِلٍ	Lesson 17	Point 8
Interrogative particles	أَدَوَاتُ الاِسْتِفْهَام	Lesson 11	Point 10
Ismul -ishaarati	اِسْمُ الإِشَارَةِ	Lesson 11	Point 8
Ismun mu'rabun	اِسْمٌ مُعْرَبٌ	Lesson 11	Point 3
Istifhaami (adawaatul-)	(أَدَوَاتُ) الاِسْتِفْهَام	Lesson 11	Point 10

172

174

177

S

179

Z

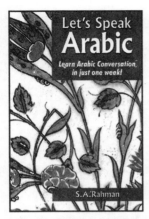

Let's Speak
Arabic
Learn Arabic Conversation
in just one week!

S.A. Rahman

INTRODUCING ARABIC

MICHAEL MUMISA

Teach Yourself
ARABIC

A MODERN AND
STEP BY STEP
APPROACH

S.A. RAHMAN

A HISTORY OF
ARABIAN MUSIC

HENRY GEORGE FARMER

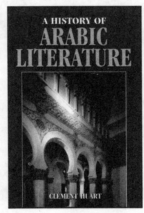

A HISTORY OF
ARABIC LITERATURE

CLEMENT HUART

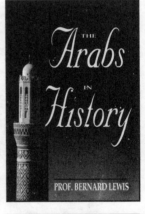

THE
Arabs
IN
History

PROF. BERNARD LEWIS

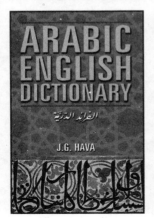

ARABIC ENGLISH DICTIONARY

J.G. HAVA

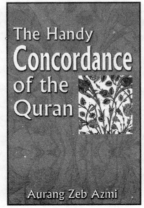

The Handy
Concordance
of the
Quran

Aurang Zeb Azmi

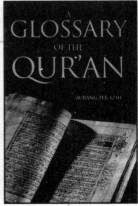

A
GLOSSARY
OF THE
QUR'AN

AURANG ZEB AZMI

Quran Challenge Game
A Fun Way to Learn About the Quran

www.goodwordbooks.com